CAMBRIDGE
Primary Science

Learner's Book 2

Jon Board & Alan Cross

CAMBRIDGE
UNIVERSITY PRESS

University Printing House, Cambridge CB2 8BS, United Kingdom

One Liberty Plaza, 20th Floor, New York, NY 10006, USA

477 Williamstown Road, Port Melbourne, VIC 3207, Australia

314–321, 3rd Floor, Plot 3, Splendor Forum, Jasola District Centre, New Delhi – 110025, India

103 Penang Road, #05–06/07, Visioncrest Commercial, Singapore 238467

Cambridge University Press is part of the University of Cambridge.

It furthers the University's mission by disseminating knowledge in the pursuit of education, learning and research at the highest international levels of excellence.

www.cambridge.org
Information on this title: www.cambridge.org/9781108742740

© Cambridge University Press 2021

This publication is in copyright. Subject to statutory exception and to the provisions of relevant collective licensing agreements, no reproduction of any part may take place without the written permission of Cambridge University Press.

First published 2014

Second edition 2021

20 19 18 17 16 15 14

Printed in Italy by L.E.G.O. S.p.A.

A catalogue record for this publication is available from the British Library

ISBN 978-1-108-74274-0 Paperback with Digital Access (1 Year)
ISBN 978-1-108-97255-0 Digital Learner's Book (1 Year)
ISBN 978-1-108-97256-7 eBook

Cambridge University Press has no responsibility for the persistence or accuracy of URLs for external or third-party internet websites referred to in this publication, and does not guarantee that any content on such websites is, or will remain, accurate or appropriate. Information regarding prices, travel timetables, and other factual information given in this work is correct at the time of first printing but Cambridge University Press does not guarantee the accuracy of such information thereafter.

Cambridge International copyright material in this publication is reproduced under licence and remains the intellectual property of Cambridge Assessment International Education.

Third-party websites and resources referred to in this publication have not been endorsed by Cambridge Assessment

NOTICE TO TEACHERS IN THE UK
It is illegal to reproduce any part of this work in material form (including photocopying and electronic storage) except under the following circumstances:
(i) where you are abiding by a licence granted to your school or institution by the Copyright Licensing Agency;
(ii) where no such licence exists, or where you wish to exceed the terms of a licence, and you have gained the written permission of Cambridge University Press;
(iii) where you are allowed to reproduce without permission under the provisions of Chapter 3 of the Copyright, Designs and Patents Act 1988, which covers, for example, the reproduction of short passages within certain types of educational anthology and reproduction for the purposes of setting examination questions.

Contents

Page	Unit	Science strand	Thinking and Working Scientifically strand	Science in Context
88	**4 Humans and animals grow**	Biology: Structure and function Biology: Life processes	Scientific enquiry: purpose and planning Scientific enquiry: carrying out scientific enquiry	Understand that we all use science and find out who uses science in their jobs.
88	4.1 Comparing animals			
94	4.2 Growing			
101	4.3 Inheriting characteristics			
106	4.4 Keeping healthy			
112	4.5 Teeth			
123	**5 Light**	Physics: Light and sound	Scientific enquiry: purpose and planning Scientific enquiry: carrying out scientific enquiry Scientific enquiry: analysis, evaluation and conclusions	Talk about how people's knowledge and understanding of science were different in the past.
123	5.1 Light sources			
130	5.2 Darkness			
137	5.3 The Sun appears to move!			
146	**6 Electricity**	Physics: Electricity and magnetism	Scientific enquiry: purpose and planning Scientific enquiry: carrying out scientific enquiry Scientific enquiry: analysis, evaluation and conclusions	Explain how an object works using science.
146	6.1 Where do we use electricity?			
152	6.2 Keep safe with electricity			
159	6.3 Making circuits			
170	**Science skills**			
175	**Glossary and index**			
185	**Acknowledgements**			

How to use this book

In this book you will find lots of different features to help your learning.

What you will learn in the topic.

We are going to:
- describe the place an animal lives as its habitat
- compare different habitats for animals
- make observations and record them in drawings.

Questions to find out what you know already.

Getting started
- Tell a friend why every living thing needs the right habitat.
- Draw a local habitat where plants live.

Important words to learn.

litter
material
nature reserve
protect
recycle

A fun activity about the Science you are learning.

Activity

Find me a habitat

Pretend you are one of the three plants in this activity.

Read the information. Then make a poster to say 'Can you find me a habitat like this?'

Rice needs a habitat which is warm, with lots of light and water. Rice grows in very wet soil.

An investigation to carry out with a partner or in groups.

Think like a scientist 1

Plants in different habitats

Go outside and look at different places around your school.

Look for plants growing in different habitats:
- against a wall
- in a shady place
- in a wet place
- in a dry pathway
- under something
- in a plant pot.

This plant is growing on a path.

Its roots have grown down a **crack** to find soil.

Take a **photograph** or draw a picture of a plant and where it is growing. You can **record** your plants and habitats like this.

How to use this book

Questions to help you think about how you learn.

> When I am learning about plants, how does it help me to observe real plants?

This is what you have learned in the topic.

Look what I can do!
- ☐ I can describe the place an animal lives as its habitat.
- ☐ I can compare different habitats for animals.
- ☐ I can make observations and record them in drawings.

Questions that cover what you have learned in the unit. If you can answer these, you are ready to move on to the next unit.

2 Which four things does the tree need in its habitat? Choose from:

soil · the Moon · water · a rainbow · the Sun · air · a plant pot

At the end of each unit, there is a project for you to carry out, using what you have learned. You might make something or solve a problem.

Project: Our school's outdoor environment

Make a small book about the environment of the school grounds.

Think about:
- habitats for plants
- habitats for animals
- where you could put an insect hotel
- ways to improve the outdoor school environment for plants and animals
- where you could put a nature reserve.

Use photographs, pictures and words to tell readers about the school grounds and the animals and plants that live there now.

Make sure you show some good habitats for animals and plants. Think of ways to improve habitats or make new ones.

How would you care for and improve the outdoor spaces around the school?

1 Environments and habitats

> 1.1 Habitats

We are going to:

- explore the environment to find the habitat of a living thing
- talk about different living things in a habitat
- compare two local habitats
- make a model of a habitat
- make observations and record them in drawings.

Getting started

- Each animal needs an **environment** which is a good **habitat** for them.
- The environment is the air, water and land where people, animals and plants live.
- Talk about the animals shown on this page and the environment they need to live in. Draw the environment needed by these animals.

compare   label
environment   model
habitat   local
home

1.1 Habitats

Each living thing needs a place to live.

We call this place the living thing's habitat.

A habitat gives the living thing everything it needs to live.

The plant's habitat is a wall. The wall is its **home**.

The plant has everything it needs to live.

It needs, light, water, soil and air.

It has a very small habitat.

The eagle's habitat is around forests and lakes. Here, the eagle finds everything it needs to live.

It needs food, water, air and a home.

It has a very large habitat.

Questions

Look at the other animals and plants in the picture.

1. What is their habitat?
2. Can they find all they need?

1 Environments and habitats

Your **local** environment has different habitats for different animals and plants.

What living things and their habitats are in this picture?

Plants grow in a habitat but they cannot move from place to place.

Animals can move in their habitat.

A spider's habitat can be in a tree.

A tree's habitat can be part of a garden.

A lizard's habitat can be a rocky place.

Activity

Habitat for a frog

A habitat for a frog might be a wet area, stream or pond.

Imagine you are a frog. What would you want to find in your habitat?

Now draw the habitat for a frog.

Label your drawing to say what each thing is.

Would this habitat be a home for other animals and for plants?

Draw these other living things in your picture.

1.1 Habitats

Think like a scientist 1

A habitat for fish

You will need:
a cardboard box, card, paper, scissors, coloured pens, glue

This tank is a habitat for fish.

Why do we call this tank a habitat?

Use a box to make a **model** of a habitat for fish.

You must give the fish everything they need.

What will you include?

Think like a scientist 2

Looking at habitats

Look at these two habitats. **Compare** them. How are they different?

Why are there more plants and animals in one habitat than in the other?

Go outside to observe your local environment.

5

1 Environments and habitats

> **Continued**
>
> Talk about what the habitat is like in one place.
>
> What plants grow? What animals might live here?
>
> Now go to a different habitat in your local environment.
>
> What plants grow? What animals might live here?
>
> Draw the two habitats and show that they are different.
>
> Add labels to your drawings.
>
> Talk to your friends about why these habitats are different.
>
> **How am I doing?**
>
> Think of a local environment where we find habitats for different animals and plants.
>
> Share your ideas with a friend.

When I learn about the world, does it help me to compare different things?

> **Look what I can do!**
> - ☐ I can explore the environment to find the habitat of a living thing.
> - ☐ I can talk about different living things in a habitat.
> - ☐ I can compare two local habitats.
> - ☐ I can make a model of a habitat.
> - ☐ I can make observations and record them in drawings.

> 1.2 Plants in different habitats

We are going to:
- describe the place a plant lives as its habitat
- describe different plants in a habitat
- compare different habitats for plants
- observe plants and record what we see in drawings and tables.

Getting started
- Tell a friend why every living thing needs the right habitat.
- Draw a local habitat where plants live.

Plants grow in many different habitats.

All plants need water. Many plants grow in or by water.

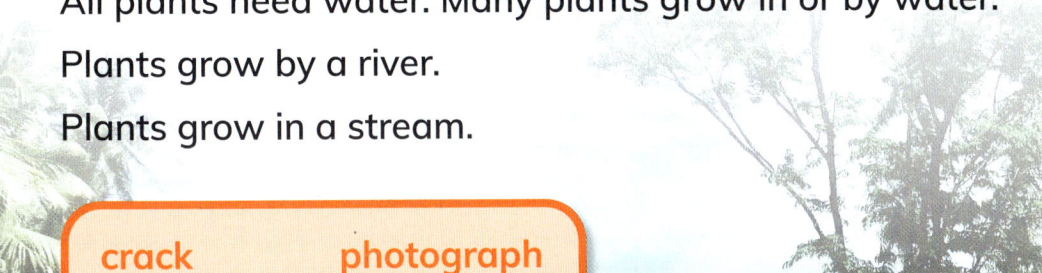

Plants grow by a river.

Plants grow in a stream.

crack   photograph
describe   pretend
desert   record

1 Environments and habitats

Some plants live in hot **deserts**.
It is very dry here.

Question

1. How can these plants live with very little water?

Think like a scientist 1

Plants in different habitats

Go outside and look at different places around your school.

Look for plants growing in different habitats:

- against a wall
- in a shady place
- in a wet place
- in a dry pathway
- under something
- in a plant pot.

This plant is growing on a path.

Its roots have grown down a **crack** to find soil.

Take a **photograph** or draw a picture of a plant and where it is growing.

You can **record** your plants and habitats like this.

1.2 Plants in different habitats

Continued

I found this plant growing in the . . .	
Here is a drawing of my plant.	It has some soil? yes/no It has water? yes/no It has light? yes/no
This habitat was . . .	

How am I doing?

Look at the records made by your friends.

Talk about the different habitats where you found plants growing.

1 Environments and habitats

Environments where plants don't grow

Different plants like different habitats.

This means that in most parts of planet Earth we find plants growing.

The pictures show places where plants don't grow.

Questions

1 Why are there no plants in these environments?
2 Think of another environment where plants cannot grow.

Activity

Find me a habitat

Pretend you are one of the three plants in this activity.

Read the information.
Then make a poster to say 'Can you find me a habitat like this?'

Rice needs a habitat which is warm, with lots of light and water. Rice grows in very wet soil.

1.2 Plants in different habitats

Continued

Pond weed needs a habitat underwater in a pond, lake or river. It needs light. It must not get very cold.

Cactus needs a habitat which is very hot. It needs light. It needs very little water.

Your poster might look like this...

Can you find me a habitat like this?

I am a...
hot, warm or cold?

I need...
water?

I need...
light?

I need...

My drawing

My habitat will look like this...

Think like a scientist 2

Finding all the plants in a habitat

You will need: a magnifying glass

Look at all the different plants which grow in a habitat.

Draw them growing in their habitat.

11

1 Environments and habitats

Continued

Use a table like this.

Drawing of the plant in its habitat	drawing of a leaf
	does it have flowers?
	drawing of a flower

Did you find plants growing on a path?

Why do plants find a path a difficult place to grow?

How am I doing?

Pretend that you are a tree.

Describe to a friend the habitat you want to live in. Are there other types of plants in your habitat?

Does your friend agree?

When I am learning about plants, how does it help me to observe real plants?

Look what I can do!

- ☐ I can describe the place a plant lives as its habitat.
- ☐ I can describe different plants in a habitat.
- ☐ I can compare different habitats for plants.
- ☐ I can observe plants and record what I see in drawings and tables.

> 1.3 Animals in different habitats

We are going to:
- describe the place an animal lives as its habitat
- compare different habitats for animals
- make observations and record them in drawings.

Getting started
- Look out of the classroom window. Talk to a friend about animals you see on the ground, in the trees or in the sky. Do you see birds, insects, animals with fur?
- Choose an animal. Describe its habitat.
- Where will it sleep?
- Where will it find food and water?
- Will it be alone?

attract
clues
droppings
egg
hide
insect
scare
table
tracks

1 Environments and habitats

All animals need a habitat, but animals may **hide** from us.

Sometimes we can tell animals are around because we see **clues**.

The clues might be **tracks**, **droppings**, leaves that have been eaten or birds singing. Sometimes we can see the animal's home.

The picture shows a tree where animals live.

Questions

1 Which animals might live in this habitat?
2 Can you see the animals?
3 Can you see any clues?
4 Why do some animals hide from us?

1.3 Animals in different habitats

Think like a scientist

Habitats for animals around school

You will need: a magnifying glass

Find somewhere in the school gardens where animals might live.

Use a magnifying glass to look for animals or **eggs**.

Remember to be quiet so that you don't **scare** the animals.

How can you tell that animals have been here?

Carefully look for leaves that have been eaten.

Record your results in a **table** like this.

Drawing of the habitat	
This animal might live here…	…because I saw…
a butterfly	it fly away

Talk about animals you saw or any clues you found.

Why were animals harder to observe than plants?

Why do animals live in this habitat?

1 Environments and habitats

Activity 1

A habitat for snails

You will need:
snails, soil, leaves, twigs, small rocks, water, plastic fish tank and lid

You must wash hands with soap and water after touching soil, leaves, twigs or snails.

Snails like to hide in cool damp places. They eat leaves and soft wood.

Make a habitat for snails in the fish tank.
Draw your ideas and then make the habitat.

Put the snails in the habitat and observe how they move and eat leaves.

Don't forget the lid or they may escape and die.

Activity 2

Let's make an insect hotel

You will need:
dry plant stems and sticks, string, scissors

You must wash hands with soap and water after touching soil, leaves, or twigs.

1.3 Animals in different habitats

Continued

Insects and other small animals need a safe place to live close to food.

Many small animals eat twigs and dead leaves.

We can make a good habitat for insects in our school grounds.

The insect hotel is made from sticks and stems. Insects love to hide in sticks - they will eat the sticks and lay eggs there.

Tie string around some stems and sticks.

Use more string to hang your insect hotel in a tree.

Now draw your insect hotel.

What sort of animals might come to live here?

What will they do in this new habitat?

If there are more insects, will this **attract** other animals?

Use books or pictures to find out about insects which might live there.

Draw some insects you hope to attract.

How am I doing?

Use modelling clay to make a small beetle or ant.

Put your model on a sheet of paper and draw the animal's habitat.

Make sure it has all it needs.

Ask a friend to look at your habitat.

Do they think it is a good habitat for the insect?

1 Environments and habitats

When I am learning about animals' habitats, does it help to visit the habitat?

Look what I can do!
- ☐ I can describe the place an animal lives as its habitat.
- ☐ I can compare different habitats for animals.
- ☐ I can make observations and record them in drawings.

> 1.4 Rocks and the environment

We are going to:
- describe and compare different rocks
- find how rocks are dug up and how this affects the environment
- sort rocks with water
- make predictions and see if they are right
- make and record observations in pictures and tables.

Getting started
- Have you seen rocks in your school or at home?
- Why have people used **rocks** here?

absorb
explosive
gravel
mine
quarry
rocks
sample
stones
swirl
waterproof

1 Environments and habitats

Using rocks

Planet Earth is made of rocks. Some rocks are deep underground, some rocks are at the surface.

We use rocks to make roads, paths, bridges, walls, floors, buildings, roofs and even fire.

Questions

1 How have rocks been used to make the things shown in these pictures?

2 What other things do we make from rocks?

1.4 Rocks and the environment

Properties of rocks

Rocks can be strong (for example, granite).

Rocks can be soft (for example, white chalk).

Rocks can be made into shapes (for example, marble).

Rocks can be **waterproof** (for example, slate).

Most rocks do not burn, but coal is a rock that burns.

Question

3 Why do we find these different properties of rocks useful?

1 Environments and habitats

Think like a scientist 1

Learning more about rocks

You will need:
samples of rocks, a paperclip

LIMESTONE
appearance
- grey, dull
size of bits
- small and some larger shapes, hard to see
hardness
- we can scratch it with metal
- we use it to build walls, buildings

COAL
appearance
- black and shiny
size of bits
- very small
hardness
- we could scratch it a little with metal
- we use it to burn to keep us warm

CHALK
appearance
- white and grey, dull
size of bits
- very small
hardness
- soft, we can scratch bits off
- we use it to write on a black board

Arun and Sofia have a **sample** of rock or a picture of a rock. They make a table about each rock.

They test the hardness of the rock by trying to scratch it with a paperclip.

Now look at your own rocks. Try scratching the rocks.

Use a table like this to record information about the rocks.

All about limestone	
Drawing	What does it look like? It is grey with some dark grey parts and some lines.

1.4 Rocks and the environment

Continued

All about limestone	
Size of bits in the rock *I can see some small bits*	We use it to… *make walls*
Hard or soft? *It is hard*	

Think like a scientist 2

Does this rock absorb water?

You will need:
a spoon, water, rock samples, magnifying glass

Tom and Mumtaz are testing rocks to see if they **absorb** water. They drip water onto the rock and observe what happens.

I think the chalk is absorbing the water.

Yes, the water goes into the chalk.

Chalk · Limestone · Slate · Sandstone · Marble

1 Environments and habitats

> **Continued**
>
> Predict what will happen when you drip water onto your rocks. Then wet them very slowly by dripping water from the spoon.
>
> Do your rocks absorb water or are the rocks waterproof?
>
> Record your results on a table like this.
>
> | | Rock | Slate |
> |---|---|---|
> | Prediction | Will it absorb water? | No |
> | Result | Did it absorb water? | No |
>
> Was your prediction right?

Digging up rocks

We dig up rocks in **quarries**, in deep **mines** and from river beds.

We use tools, diggers, trucks and trains to dig and move the heavy rocks.

Quarry

A quarry is a place where we dig rock at the Earth's surface. Sometimes we use **explosives** to break rock into pieces. This is a dangerous job.

Rocks we get from a quarry are limestone, marble, slate and sandstone.

Deep mine

A deep mine is a place where we dig up rock deep underground. People use spades and other tools. This is very dangerous work.

Rocks we get from mines are coal, marble, salt.

1.4 Rocks and the environment

River bed

A river bed is a place where we dig **stones**. We use spades and big diggers.

From rivers we dig sand, **gravel** and pebbles.

When people dig up rocks they damage the environment. Trees and other plants are killed, animals are killed and lose their homes. Look at this picture. There was once a forest, a home for hundreds of animals and plants, now there is a hole with only a few animals and plants living there.

Question

4 Close your eyes and think about working in a mine. It would be dirty, hot and dangerous. What might you see?

Using water to sort stones

We can use water to sort small rocks. A stone is another name for a small rock.

The moving water in the bowl sorts lighter, smaller stones from the larger, heavier stones.

25

1 Environments and habitats

Think like a scientist 3

Sorting stones with water

> **You will need:**
> a bowl of water and some stones or soil

Draw your bowl with stones or soil in it.

Predict what will happen when you add and move the water.

Add water and **swirl** the water.
You will see the small pieces sorted by the water.

How am I doing?

Pretend you discover rocks with gold in them under your school playground. Talk to a friend about how people could get the rocks.

When learning science, does it help you to close your eyes and imagine things?

Look what I can do!

- ☐ I can describe and compare different rocks.
- ☐ I can talk about how rocks are dug up and how this affects the environment.
- ☐ I can sort rocks with water.
- ☐ I can make predictions and see if they were right.
- ☐ I can make and record observations in pictures and tables.

> 1.5 How can we care for our environment?

We are going to:
- find out about how people can change the environment
- make observations and record them in pictures and tables
- make predictions and see if they are right.

Getting started
- Have you seen **litter** where you live?
  Tell a friend about what you have seen.
- Draw an animal which might be hurt by litter.

litter
material
nature reserve
protect
recycle

27

1 Environments and habitats

People can affect the environment. We build many things like houses, roads and bridges. We plant trees and even new forests. We can do good and bad things for the environment.

This beach is covered in litter. Dirty water comes from the pipe.

Litter is bad for animals and plants.

Questions

1. How can this litter harm the animals and plants?
2. What can we do to protect the animals and plants shown in the picture?

Activity 1

Litter

Go outside and look for places where people have not cared for the environment.

1.5 How can we care for our environment?

Continued

Write, draw or photograph what you see.

1 How could people care for the environment better?
2 Why do people drop litter?
3 What could you do to help? Talk about your ideas.

Make a poster to show your ideas.

These children are helping to **protect** the environment.

Questions

1 What are the children in the picture doing?
2 Which materials can you **recycle** in school?

1 Environments and habitats

Activity 2

Making a nature reserve

We can improve the environment and make better habitats for animals and plants.

These children are looking at their school garden. It has not been cared for.

There are few plants and animals.

The children want to make this place into a **nature reserve**.

Plan how to make a nature reserve. It must be a good habitat for plants and animals. Write and draw your ideas.

1.5 How can we care for our environment?

Think like a scientist

Survey the environment

Remember that litter can be dangerous, so talk to an adult before you pick up litter.

Predict whether places in the school grounds will be good for living things.

Now look around the school grounds. Perhaps you can also visit places outside school.

Look for a good habitat for plants and animals. Do you see litter? Make notes like this.

Place	Predict – is this a good place for living things?	Is it a good habitat?	Is there litter?	How could we improve this place?
school car park area	no	no – there are no plants	paper and plastic	we can remove the litter and sow some seeds
street outside school	no	no – there is only one tree	card and paper	we could plant a tree
school allotment	yes	yes – there are many plants and animals	no	we could grow plants here for the school car park

1 Environments and habitats

Continued

Talk about the things you found. Were your predictions right?

Could you do things to help the animals and plants?

Who might help you?

How am I doing?

Could you make the area around your home better?
Tell a friend what you could do to improve your local environment.

When I am learning about the environment, does it help me to go outside and look for myself?

Look what I can do!

- ☐ I can talk about ways that people can change the environment.
- ☐ I can record my observations with drawings and tables.
- ☐ I can make predictions and see if they are right.

Project: Our school's outdoor environment

Project: Our school's outdoor environment

In this project you will see how people can have a positive effect on the environment. Make a small book about the environment of the school grounds.

Think about:

- habitats for plants
- habitats for animals
- where you could put an insect hotel
- ways to improve the outdoor school environment for plants and animals
- where you could put a nature reserve.

Use photographs, pictures and words to tell readers about the school grounds and the animals and plants that live there now.

Make sure you show some good habitats for animals and plants. Think of ways to improve habitats or make new ones.

How would you care for and improve the outdoor spaces around the school?

33

1 Environments and habitats

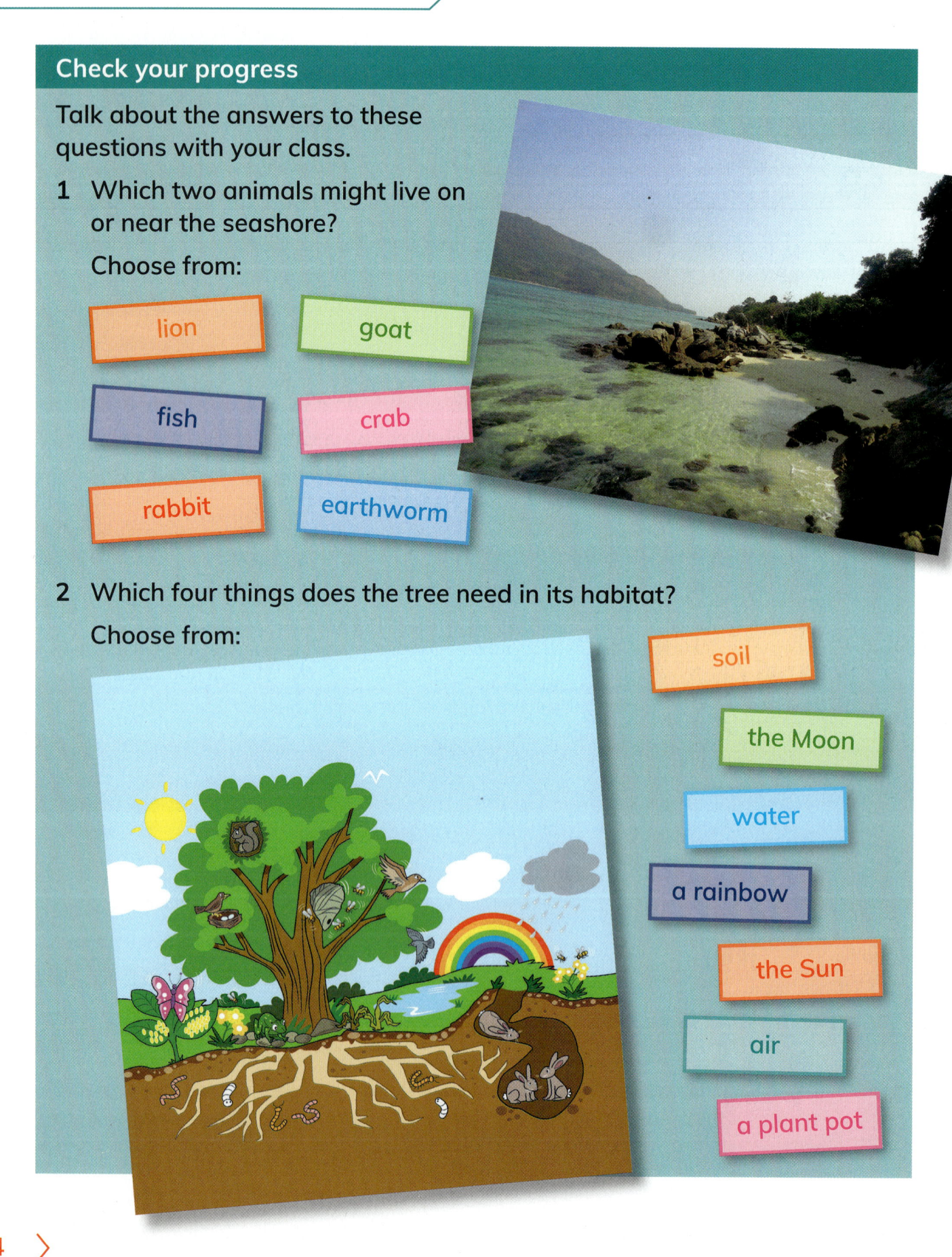

Check your progress

Talk about the answers to these questions with your class.

1. Which two animals might live on or near the seashore?

   Choose from:
   - lion
   - goat
   - fish
   - crab
   - rabbit
   - earthworm

2. Which four things does the tree need in its habitat?

   Choose from:
   - soil
   - the Moon
   - water
   - a rainbow
   - the Sun
   - air
   - a plant pot

Check your progress

Continued

3 a Where does this woman work?

    b What tools might she use?

    c What rock might she dig up?

4 Why do we use slate for roofs?

5 Why do people make nature reserves?

2 Forces and movement

> 2.1 Forces around us

We are going to:
- learn that forces can make things move and make things stop
- make predictions and say if they are right
- work in a safe way.

away	rocket
force	squashing
launch	stretch
pull/pulls	towards
push/pushes	

Getting started
- Tell a friend about things that you move at home.
- Do you have to **push** them or **pull** them to make them move?
- Show a friend something that moves when you push it.
- Now show them something that moves when you pull it.

2.1 Forces around us

Pushes and pulls are **forces**.

A push is a force **away** from you.

A pull is a force **towards** you.

This girl is pushing.

These boys are pulling.

Forces can make things move and they can make things stop.

This man uses a push to stop the ball.

2 Forces and movement

Activity

Using forces to move things and stop things

You will need:
a ball, a bowl of water, a balloon, a chair and a pencil

How can you make a ball move?

Will the ball move if you push it?

Will it move if you pull it?

How can you make it stop?

Try making the other things move and making them stop.

Be careful of other people. Make sure you work in a safe way with the ball.

2.1 Forces around us

There are small forces and big forces.

Omar pulls his toys with elastic. The elastic can stretch.

Questions

1 Which toy needs a big pull to make it move?
2 Which toy needs a small pull to make it move?
3 This man is pulling a big rock.
   Do you think the rock will move?

39

2 Forces and movement

Think like a scientist

Make a paper rocket launcher

You will need:
some paper and a plastic bottle

Zara has made a **rocket**. She can **launch** it by **squashing** the bottle with a push.

Make your own paper rocket.
Look at the pictures to see what to do.

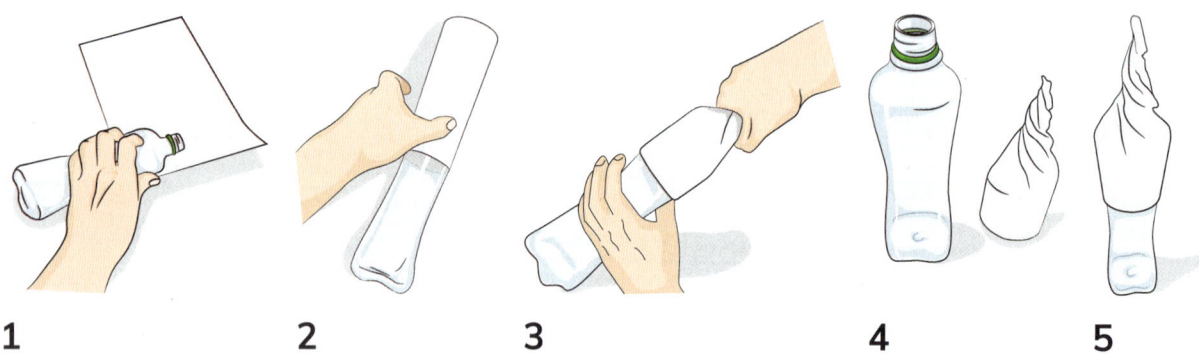

1 2 3 4 5

Use a small push to launch your rocket. Then use a big push.

Launch your rocket from the floor.

Predict how high the rocket will go each time.
Use your hand to show how high you think your rocket will go.

What happens when you use a small push?

How is it different when you use a big push?

Were your predictions correct?

Remember to work safely. Do not launch your rocket towards people.

How am I doing?

Ask a friend to predict how high their rocket will go. Watch them launch their rocket. Can they say if their prediction was correct?

2.1 Forces around us

Which of your five senses can you use to observe forces? Can you use more than one sense?

Look what I can do!

- ☐ I can say how a push or pull can make things move or make things stop.
- ☐ I can make predictions and say if they are correct.
- ☐ I can work in a safe way.

2 Forces and movement

> 2.2 Changing shape

We are going to:
- learn that forces can change the shape of some objects
- use objects to measure
- look for patterns in our results
- record our results in a table.

Getting started
- What do you do that changes the **shape** of things?
- Say how you change the shape of each thing.
- Make a list with your class.

> How do we change the shape of things?
> - chewing food
> - folding clothes

2.2 Changing shape

Look at these **objects**.

We can change the shape of the objects.

We can use forces to make bread.

We can use forces to make clay into the shape of a pot.

We can use forces to change the shape of wood.

height	pattern
investigate	results
measure	shape
object	

Think like a scientist 1

Finding patterns in results

> **You will need:**
> a ball of soft clay and some counting bricks

Drop a ball made from soft clay.

Count the bricks to **measure** the **height** you drop the ball from.

Observe how the shape of the ball changes.

Make the clay back into a ball and drop it again from a different height.

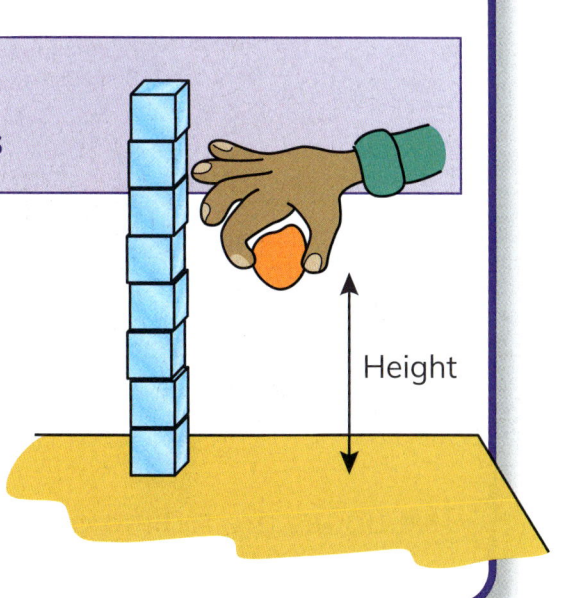

Height

43

2 Forces and movement

Continued

Record your **results** by writing or drawing in a table like this one.

Height	Result
2 bricks	
4 bricks	
6 bricks	
8 bricks	

How does the result change for the different heights?

Is there a **pattern**?

A pattern in results is when there is a similar change in the result each time.

Use the pattern to predict what will happen if you drop the ball from a height of 10 bricks.

Think like a scientist 2

How forces can change rubber bands

You will need:
some books, a big rubber band, sticky notes, 2 small rubber bands and a paperclip

Look at the pictures to see what to do.

The books are pulling on the rubber band.

44

2.2 Changing shape

Continued

Investigate what happens to the rubber band when there is a bigger pull.

Use the sticky notes to measure the length of the rubber band.

Record your results in a table like this.

Number of books	Number of sticky notes
0	1
1	
2	
3	

Try to find the pattern in your results.

How am I doing?

Check your friends' measurements.
Have they measured the length of the rubber band correctly?

Did you add one book each time?

Was that a good way to do take the measurements?

Lola has done an investigation to see how forces change rubber bands. Here are her results.

Number of books	Number of sticky notes
0	1
3	4
1	2
2	3

There is no pattern in my results.

2 Forces and movement

Questions

1 Lola is wrong. Can you see why?
2 Why is it a good idea to add one book each time?

Look what I can do!
☐ I can say how forces can change the shape of some objects.
☐ I can use objects to measure.
☐ I can find patterns in my results.
☐ I can record my results in a table.

> 2.3 Changing speed

> **We are going to:**
> - find out how forces make things go faster or slower
> - ask questions about how to make things go faster or slower
> - look for patterns in our results
> - investigate carefully and safely.

Getting started

Mia has a new bike.
- How can she go faster?
- How can she go slower?
- Tell your friends what you think.

brakes	slow
explain	slower
fast	slow down
faster	speed
pedals	speed up

To go **faster** on a bike you push on the **pedals**.

To go **slower** you pull on the **brakes**.

Going faster is called **speeding up**.
Going slower is called **slowing down**.

Your **speed** is how **fast** you are moving.

When something speeds up or slows down it is because of a force.

Question

1 How can you make other things speed up or **slow** down?

2 Forces and movement

Think like a scientist 1

Asking questions about speed

You will need:
some sticky notes

Look at the children in the park.

Dai uses some cards to make a question.

Do you know the answer?

Think of some other questions about speed.

Talk about how to find out the answers with your friends.

How do you make... Go faster? Go slower?

2.3 Changing speed

Did you find it easy to think of questions about speed?
Asking questions is an important part of science.
Can you ask any other science questions?

Think like a scientist 2

Blow the ball

You will need:
a ball

Sofia and Marcus are trying to make a ball speed up and slow down.

Marcus pushes the ball towards Sofia. Sofia blows towards the ball. The air pushes the ball to make it go slower.

2 Forces and movement

Continued

How can they make the ball go faster without touching it?

Try doing this with a ball.

Try to make the ball slow down and speed up.

Make sure you use the ball safely.

> The bigger the push, the …

Sofia thinks there is a pattern in how the ball moves.

Try to help her explain the pattern.

How am I doing?

Watch some friends as they blow a ball. Are they being safe?

Observe the ball carefully.

Can they make the ball slow down? Can they make it speed up?

A bowling ball needs to have lots of speed to knock over the pins.

Question

2 How would you make a bowling ball go fast?

2.3 Changing speed

Look what I can do!

- ☐ I can say how forces can make something move faster or slower.
- ☐ I can ask questions about how to make something move faster or slower.
- ☐ I can find patterns in my results.
- ☐ I can investigate carefully and safely.

2 Forces and movement

> 2.4 Changing direction

We are going to:
- find out how forces make things change direction
- predict what we think will happen
- say if our predictions are correct or not
- find out how a diagram is different to a picture.

diagram
direction
turn

Getting started
- Adjo is being pulled along. What is going to happen?
- How can Adjo not crash?

2.4 Changing direction

When you are going one way and then you **turn** to go a different way you change **direction**.

Forces are needed to make things change direction.

This boat has pushed the water to make it turn.

Activity

Feel the force

The children are playing a running game.

They have to change direction when someone says 'Change'.

Try playing this game.

How do you change direction?

Can you feel the forces you use?

2 Forces and movement

Think like a scientist

This way or that way?

> **You will need:**
> a ball, a large piece of paper and two coloured marker pens

Arun and Zara are investigating how a ball changes direction when they push it.

They make a **diagram** to show their prediction. A diagram is different from a picture. Diagrams only show the things that are important. They have labels and arrows.

Arun and Zara then test their prediction.

Was their prediction correct?

Try doing this investigation.

Draw a diagram to show your prediction and your result. Use a different colour for your prediction.

How am I doing?

Have a look at your friends' diagrams.

Can they say if their predictions were correct or not?

2.4 Changing direction

Sometimes, when a prediction is wrong you learn something new.
Were your predictions correct?
What did you learn?

These people are playing wheelchair basketball.

Question

1   How can they make the wheelchairs change direction?

Look what I can do!
- ☐ I can say how forces can make something change direction.
- ☐ I can predict what I think will happen.
- ☐ I can say if my predictions are correct or not.
- ☐ I can say how a diagram is different to a picture.

2 Forces and movement

Project: How people use forces

Paco is a school caretaker.

How does he use forces to look after the school?

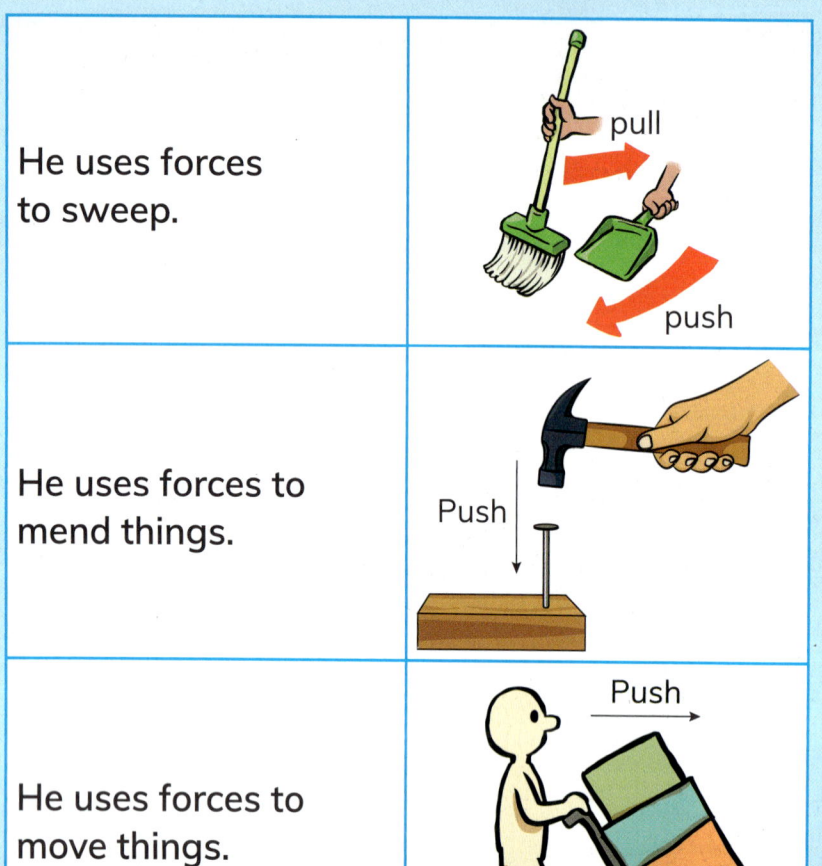

He uses forces to sweep.	pull / push
He uses forces to mend things.	Push
He uses forces to move things.	Push

Are there other people who use forces in your school?

Do you have a cook, a cleaner or a gardener who use forces?

Do the learners and teachers use forces?

Choose some people in your school and make a list of the different ways they use forces.

Draw pictures of them or photograph them using forces.

Label the pushes and pulls used in your drawings.

Check your progress

Talk about the answers to these questions with your classmates.

1. Is this girl pulling or pushing? How do you know?

2. Here is a ball bouncing towards Kamili.
   a. How can she stop it?
   b. How can she make it change direction?

2 Forces and movement

Continued

3 Vishni and Chipo are riding bicycles.

   a How can Chipo go faster?

   b How can Vishni slow down?

   c How can they change direction?

4 In this picture, the ball is moving fast across the goal from left to right.

   Nico will kick the ball with a small force.

   He makes a prediction.

   Is his prediction correct?

If I kick the ball straight at the net, I will score a goal!

3 Getting materials right

> 3.1 Natural and made materials

We are going to:
- learn about where materials come from
- learn which materials are natural and which materials have been made by people
- use books, videos or the internet to answer questions.

Getting started
- Do you know what paper is made from?
- What other materials can you see in this picture?
- Do all materials have to be made?
- Talk to a friend about where these materials come from.

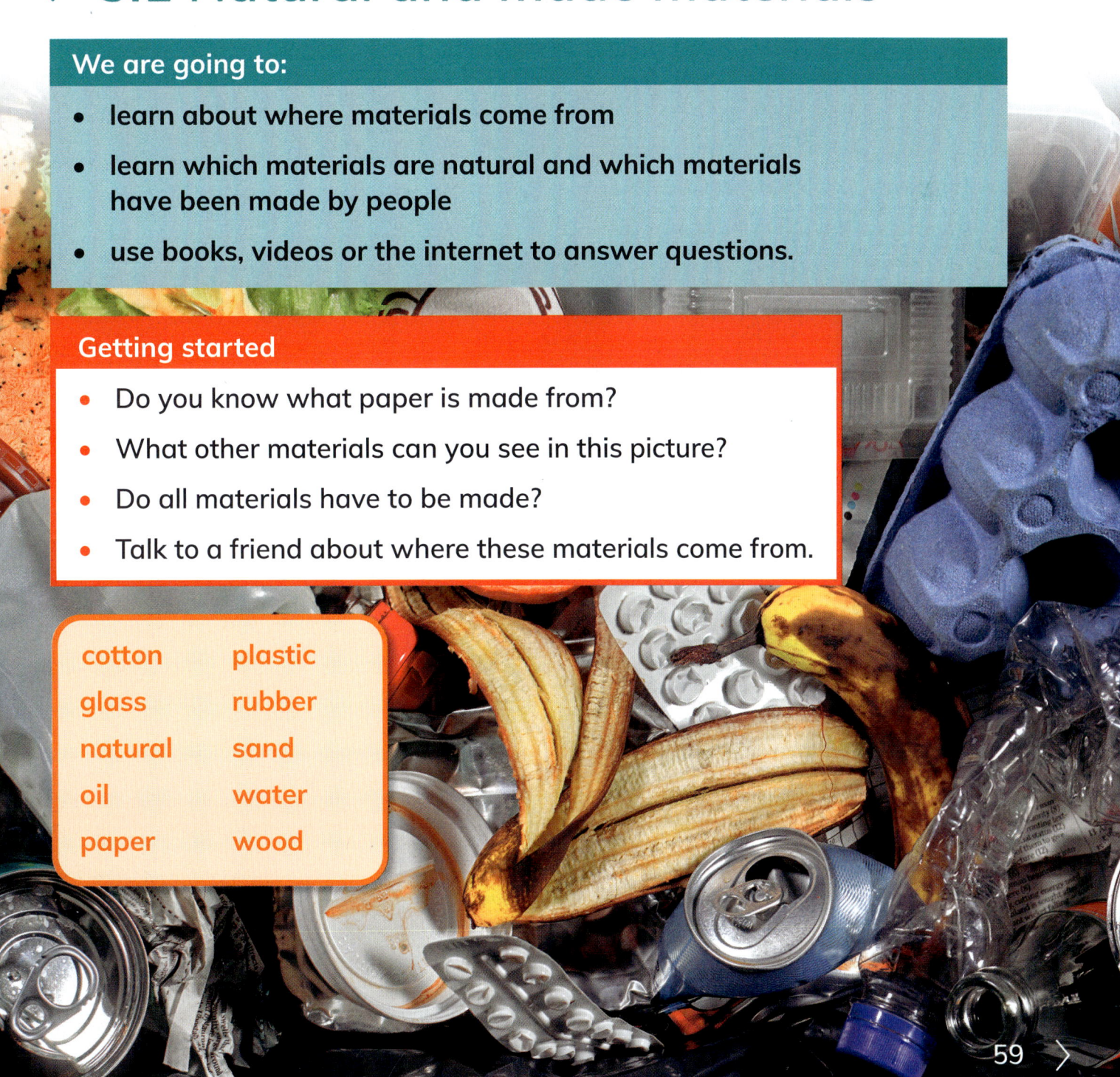

cotton	plastic
glass	rubber
natural	sand
oil	water
paper	wood

3 Getting materials right

There are many **natural** materials. They come from the world around us. The materials in these pictures are natural.

Wood is natural.

Sand is natural.

Rock is natural.

Water is natural.

This woman is getting **rubber** from a rubber tree. Rubber is natural.

Oil is natural.
Oil comes from underground.

3.1 Natural and made materials

Other materials have to be made by people.

Paper is made from wood.

Glass is made from sand.

Plastic is made from oil.

Questions

1. Where does wood come from?
2. Is rock a natural material or a made material?
3. Name a type of rock.
4. What else can we use rubber for?

Activity

Natural or made materials?

Look around your school for different materials.

Talk about the materials you find.

Where do they come from?

Are they natural or made?

Draw and label the materials and where they come from.

How am I doing?

Look at a friend's work. Tell them if you think they are right or wrong.

3 Getting materials right

Think like a scientist

Finding out where materials come from

You will need:
a book, website or video about how materials are made

Cotton is a fabric used to make many clothes.

Where does cotton come from?

Try to find the answer in this book.

Cotton

Cotton is a natural material. It grows on a plant

Cotton growing

Cotton factory

The cotton is picked and made into fabric in a factory. The fabric is used to make t-shirts and other clothes

Use a book, website or video to find out where other materials come from.

You could try to find out more about rubber, plastic, glass or oil.

Draw and label pictures like this to record what you find out.

Cotton grows on a plant → It is made into fabric in a factory → It is used to make clothes

3.1 Natural and made materials

We can answer science questions in different ways.
We used a book to find the answer to the question about cotton.
Think of a different way to find the answer to this question:
Is cotton fabric waterproof?

Look what I can do!

- ☐ I can say where some materials come from.
- ☐ I can name two or more natural materials and two or more materials that have been made.
- ☐ I can use a book, video or the internet to answer questions.

3 Getting materials right

> 3.2 Properties of materials

We are going to:
- learn about the properties of different materials
- learn that materials have more than one property
- ask questions about materials and find answers by observing
- put materials into groups using their properties.

Getting started
- How many different **properties** of materials can you think of? Make a list.
- Try to name a material that has each property.

absorbent
characteristic
dull
flexible
property/properties
rigid
rough
shiny
smooth
strong
Venn diagram
weak

3.2 Properties of materials

Rock is **rigid** but rubber can be **flexible**.

Water cannot get through plastic.
Plastic is waterproof.

Water soaks into most fabric.
Most fabric is absorbent.

The properties of materials tell us what a material is like.
The properties of a material are also called the **characteristics** of the material.

Materials have many different characteristics.

3 Getting materials right

Metal is **strong** but it has other characteristics.

Questions

1. Is metal waterproof or **absorbent**?
2. What other characteristics does metal have?

Think like a scientist 1

Questions about materials

You will need:
some objects made of different materials

Here is a question about a material.
Is paper strong or **weak**?

You can find the answer by testing paper.

Paper is weak.

3.2 Properties of materials

Continued

Some materials may be sharp when broken. Do not touch sharp edges.

Here is another question. Is paper **smooth** or **rough**?

You can find the answer by observing paper.

Does it look smooth or rough? How does it feel?

Ask your own questions about materials.

Find the answers by testing or observing the material.

Record your results in a table like this.

		Questions	
Material	Is it strong or weak?	Is it smooth or rough?	
paper	weak	smooth	

How am I doing?

Compare your results with others. Do you have the same answers?

If not, you could observe or test the materials again.

Think like a scientist 2

Using a Venn diagram for sorting

You will need:
some objects made of different materials and a **Venn diagram**.

We can use the properties of materials to sort them.

3 Getting materials right

Continued

Sofia and Arun are using a Venn diagram to sort some objects.

The metal key is **shiny** but not flexible.
It goes in the circle labelled 'shiny'.

The writing paper is **dull**, not shiny and it is flexible.
It goes in the circle labelled 'flexible'.

The plastic bottle is shiny and flexible. It goes in both circles.

Where should the glass bottle go?

Choose two different characteristics of materials and use a Venn diagram to sort some objects.

How am I doing?

Ask a friend to look at your Venn diagram.

Is everything in the right circle?

If not, can they tell you why?

3.2 Properties of materials

How is using a Venn diagram more useful than sorting things into two different groups?

Look what I can do!

- ☐ I can talk about the properties of four or more materials.
- ☐ I can name two or more properties of some materials.
- ☐ I can ask a question about a material and show how to find the answer.
- ☐ I can use properties to sort materials into groups.

3 Getting materials right

> 3.3 Using the right material

We are going to:
- find out why a material can be good for making some objects but not others
- record our observations in a table.

Getting started
- Why are windows made of glass?
- Could a window be made of a different material?
- Talk to a friend about your ideas.

> transparent

Every material has properties or characteristics. The characteristics make the material good for making some objects, but not others. Glass is good for a window because it is **transparent**. This means we can see through it.

3.3 Using the right material

Wood is hard and strong. We can make wood into chairs and tables.

Plastic is waterproof and comes in many colours. We can make plastic into cups and bottles.

Metal is strong and can be sharp. We make metal into knives, forks and spoons.

Metal is a sensible material for a bike because of the properties of metal.

Rubber is a silly material for a bike.

Questions

1. What would happen if a bike was made of rubber?
2. What would happen to a table made of chocolate?

Activity 1

Sensible and silly materials

Draw an object made of a silly material and the same object made of a sensible material.

Talk about the properties that make the materials silly or sensible for your object. Add labels to your pictures to show the properties.

3 Getting materials right

Activity 2

Why is that material useful?

Find objects that are made of only one material.

Talk about why each object is made of that material.

Record your observations and ideas in a table like this.

Object	Material	Useful properties of that material
chair	plastic	Strong so does not break. Flexible to make it comfortable. Light so it is easy to move.

Sam has another property of plastic that she thinks is useful for a chair. Do you think she is right?

> Plastic is good for a chair because it is waterproof.

Sam is not right. Plastic is waterproof but we do not need a waterproof material to make an indoor chair.

How am I doing?

Have a look at the properties in your table.
Are they all needed to make the object?

Look what I can do!

☐ I can say why a material has been used to make an object.

☐ I can record observations in a table.

3.4 Testing materials

We are going to:
- learn that we can test materials to find out their properties
- make predictions
- use bricks or counters to measure
- use and make a block graph.

Getting started
- How do you know if a fabric is waterproof?
- Look at the fabric of your clothes. Is the fabric waterproof?
- What could you do to find out?
- Talk about your ideas with your class.

block graph

73

3 Getting materials right

We can test things to find out their properties.

We can try to bend materials to find out if they are flexible.

We can test fabrics to find out if they are waterproof or absorbent.

Is this umbrella waterproof or absorbent?

Testing cushions

Zara and Marcus want to know which cushion is the softest.

They put a rock on each cushion to see how far it goes down.

They use a ruler and some bricks to measure how far down the rock goes.

Zara and Marcus make a **block graph** of their results.

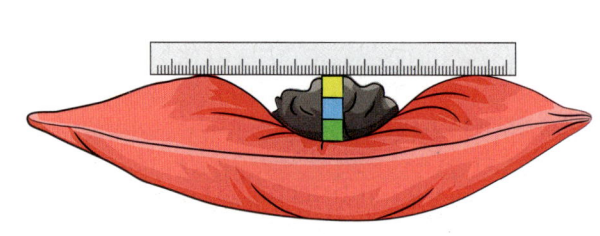

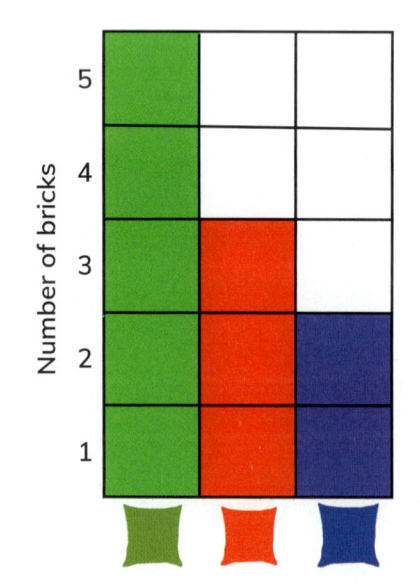

Questions

1 Which cushion is the softest?

2 Which cushion is the hardest?

3.4 Testing materials

Think like a scientist 1

Which fabric is best for an umbrella?

> **You will need:**
> some different fabrics and some water

An umbrella needs to be waterproof.

Predict which fabric will be most waterproof.

Put a small drop of water onto each fabric and observe what happens.

If the water stays on top the fabric is waterproof.

If the water is absorbed the fabric is absorbent.

Use your observations to sort the fabrics into a table like this.

Waterproof	Absorbent

Were your predictions correct?

75

3 Getting materials right

Think like a scientist 2

Which paper makes the strongest bag?

> **You will need:**
> some different types of paper, a paperclip, a rubber band, a pencil and some plastic bricks or counters

Look at different types of paper.

Predict which paper is the strongest.

Look at the pictures to see how to test the paper.

Use the bricks to measure how long the rubber band is when the paper tears.

Make a block graph of your results.

Were your predictions correct?

Which paper would make the strongest bag?

Do not stretch the rubber bands too much. They could break and hurt people.

How am I doing?

Compare your results with others. If they are not the same you may need to test the paper again to check.

3.4 Testing materials

Sometimes it can be difficult to measure correctly. What can you do if you are not sure your measurement is correct?

Look what I can do!

- ☐ I can test materials to find out their properties.
- ☐ I can make a prediction.
- ☐ I can measure using bricks or counters.
- ☐ I can use and make a block graph.

3 Getting materials right

3.5 Changing materials

We are going to:
- find out how to change some materials
- ask questions and talk about how to find out the answers
- make labelled diagrams
- learn how a diagram is different to a picture.

Getting started
- Think of a way to change a material so it has different properties.
- How is this wood being changed?
- How can ice be changed?
- Draw your ideas. Then talk about them with your class.

information
liquid
melt
mixture
solid

78

3.5 Changing materials

Making a cake

Arun is making a cake. He has some **solid** materials: flour, sugar, butter and chocolate. He breaks some eggs. These are a **liquid**.

He changes these materials to make the cake.

First, he makes a **mixture** of three different materials.

He mixes the sugar and butter together, then adds the eggs.

Next, he makes the chocolate **melt** by making it hot.

The solid chocolate changes into liquid chocolate.

79

3 Getting materials right

> Then he adds the liquid chocolate and the flour to his mixture.

> Now he heats the mixture in the oven.
> The heat makes the liquid egg change into a new solid material. This new material holds the other materials together so the cake can keep its shape.

Questions

1. Which material changed from a solid to a liquid when it was heated?
2. Which material changed from a liquid to a solid when it was heated?

When we heat liquid egg, we make a new material.
The new solid material cannot be changed back into liquid egg.

Heating solid chocolate only changes the properties of chocolate. The liquid chocolate can be made back into solid chocolate by making it cold.

3.5 Changing materials

Think like a scientist 1

Observing toast

You will need:
some bread and a magnifying glass

- Yellow crumbs
- Small holes
- Brown crumbs
- Crust

This is a picture of some bread.   This is a diagram of some bread.

A diagram is like a picture but it only shows the important **information**.

A diagram has labels to show more information.

Here the diagram does not show the knife or the cutting board because we are only learning about the bread.

Observe some bread carefully. Use a magnifying glass to see closely.

Is it flexible or rigid?

Draw a diagram of what the bread looks like.

Label your diagram.

Your teacher will now heat the bread in a grill or a toaster.

What do you predict will happen?

Do not touch the toaster or grill. They get very hot.

Observe what happens to the bread. Use the magnifying glass again. Draw another diagram to show how the material has changed.

3 Getting materials right

Continued

The bread has been changed into a new material that has different properties.

The new material is a different colour and it is harder and more rigid than the bread.

It tastes different, too.

Think like a scientist 2

Can you stop peeled fruit going brown?

You will need:
some peeled fruit and some different liquids

When you peel an apple or a banana it starts to turn brown.

Air makes the material of the apple change into a new material.

Jun has a question.

How can Jun find out the answer to her question?

Talk about your ideas with a friend.

Will water stop my apple from going brown?

3.5 Changing materials

> **Continued**
>
> Look at the things you can investigate.
>
> What might stop the fruit going brown?
>
> Ask your own question 'Will _____ stop my fruit from going brown?'
>
> How will you find out the answer to your question?
>
> Draw a diagram to show what you will do in your investigation.
>
> Now try your investigation and draw a diagram of the result.
>
> Remember to label the important things in the diagram.
>
> **How am I doing?**
>
> Look at a friend's question and their diagram.
> Did their investigation find out the answer to their question?
> Tell them what you think.

Why is a diagram often more useful than a picture?
How does a diagram help you to learn?

Look what I can do!

☐ I can describe how some materials can be changed.
☐ I can ask a question and talk about how to find out the answer.
☐ I can draw and label a diagram.
☐ I can say how a diagram is different from a picture.

3 Getting materials right

Project: Materials can damage the Earth

We know that paper is made from wood. Trees are cut down to make paper. This is bad for forests and for the animals and plants that live in forest habitats.

But we can recycle used paper to make new paper. This saves trees.

We know that plastic is made from oil. Oil comes from underground. Getting the oil out causes pollution. Used plastic is often dropped as litter. There is now lots of plastic pollution in our rivers and in the sea.

But we can recycle used plastic to make new plastic. This mean less pollution.

Project: Materials can damage the Earth

Continued

Science teaches us that we are damaging our world.

Science teaches us that we should use recycled paper and plastic and we should not drop litter.

Use books or the internet to find out some other things we should do to help our planet.

Make a poster to tell others how they can help save planet Earth.

Tell people:

- how they can save trees
- how they can make less pollution
- why they should not drop litter.

3 Getting materials right

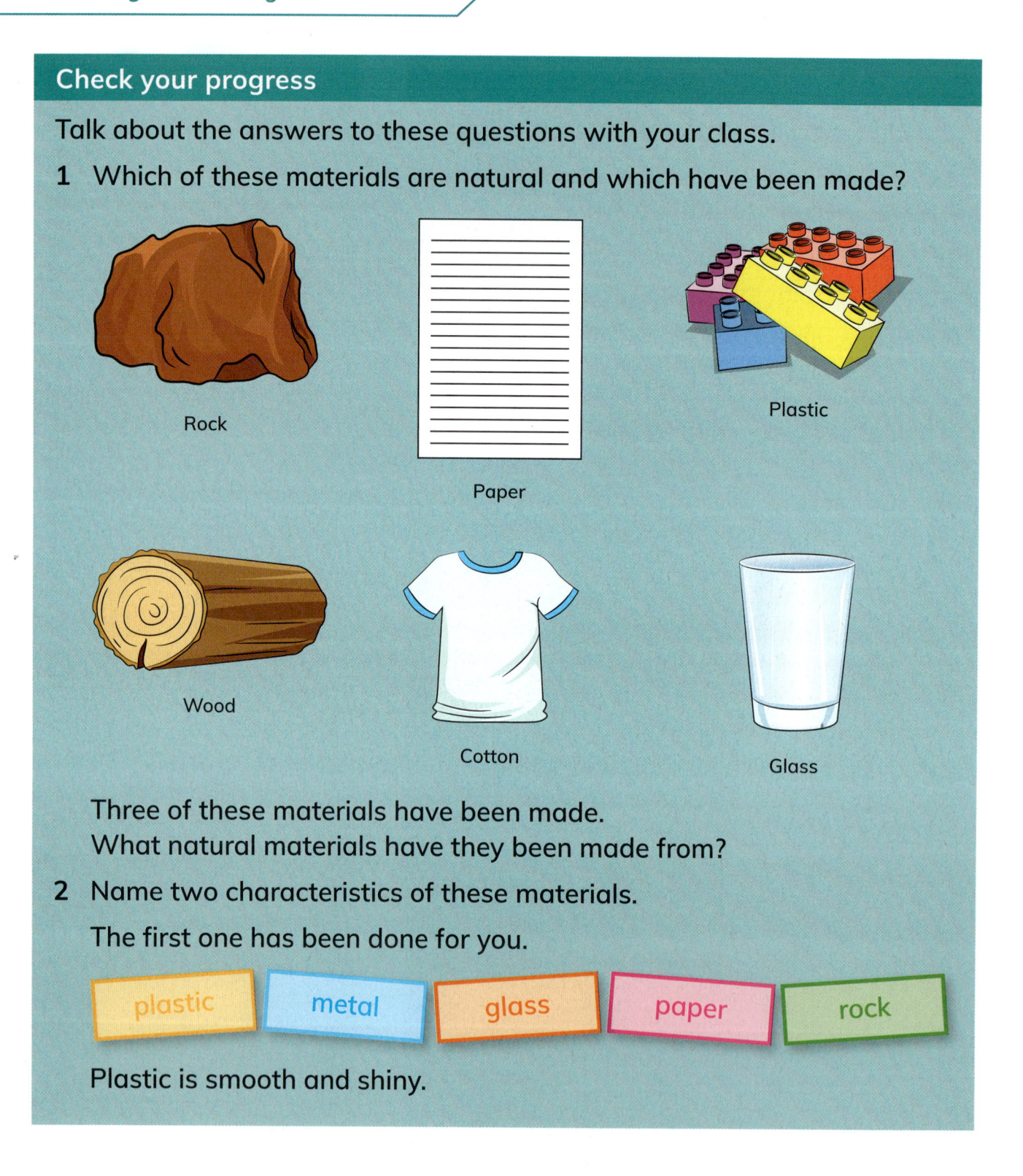

Check your progress

Talk about the answers to these questions with your class.

1. Which of these materials are natural and which have been made?

Rock

Paper

Plastic

Wood

Cotton

Glass

Three of these materials have been made.
What natural materials have they been made from?

2. Name two characteristics of these materials.
   The first one has been done for you.

   | plastic | metal | glass | paper | rock |

   Plastic is smooth and shiny.

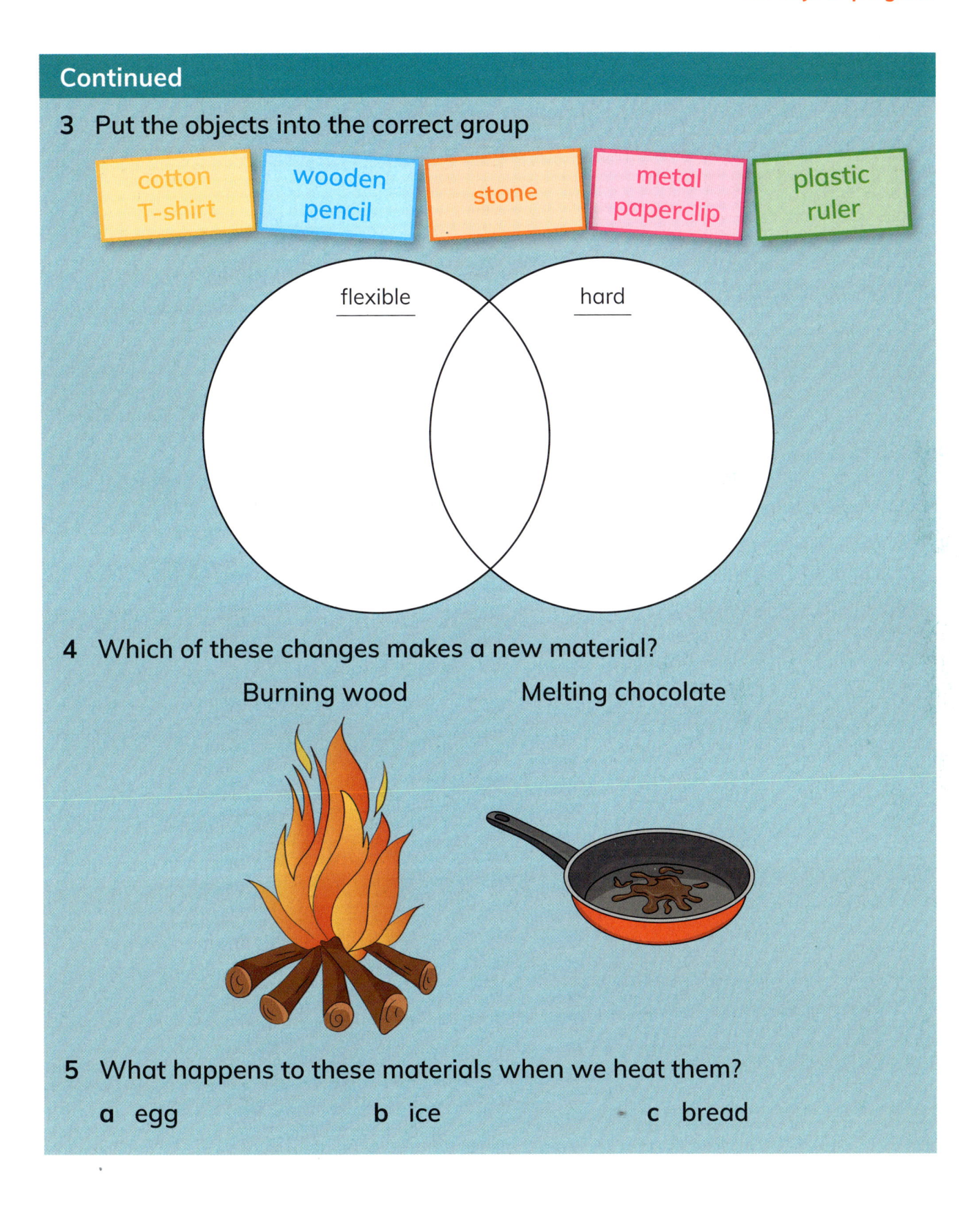

Continued

3 Put the objects into the correct group

cotton T-shirt   wooden pencil   stone   metal paperclip   plastic ruler

flexible   hard

4 Which of these changes makes a new material?

      Burning wood   Melting chocolate

5 What happens to these materials when we heat them?

   a egg   b ice   c bread

4 > Humans and animals grow

> 4.1 Comparing animals

We are going to:
- find out how animals look similar and different
- ask our own questions about animals
- use books, videos or the internet to answer questions
- use and make block graphs.

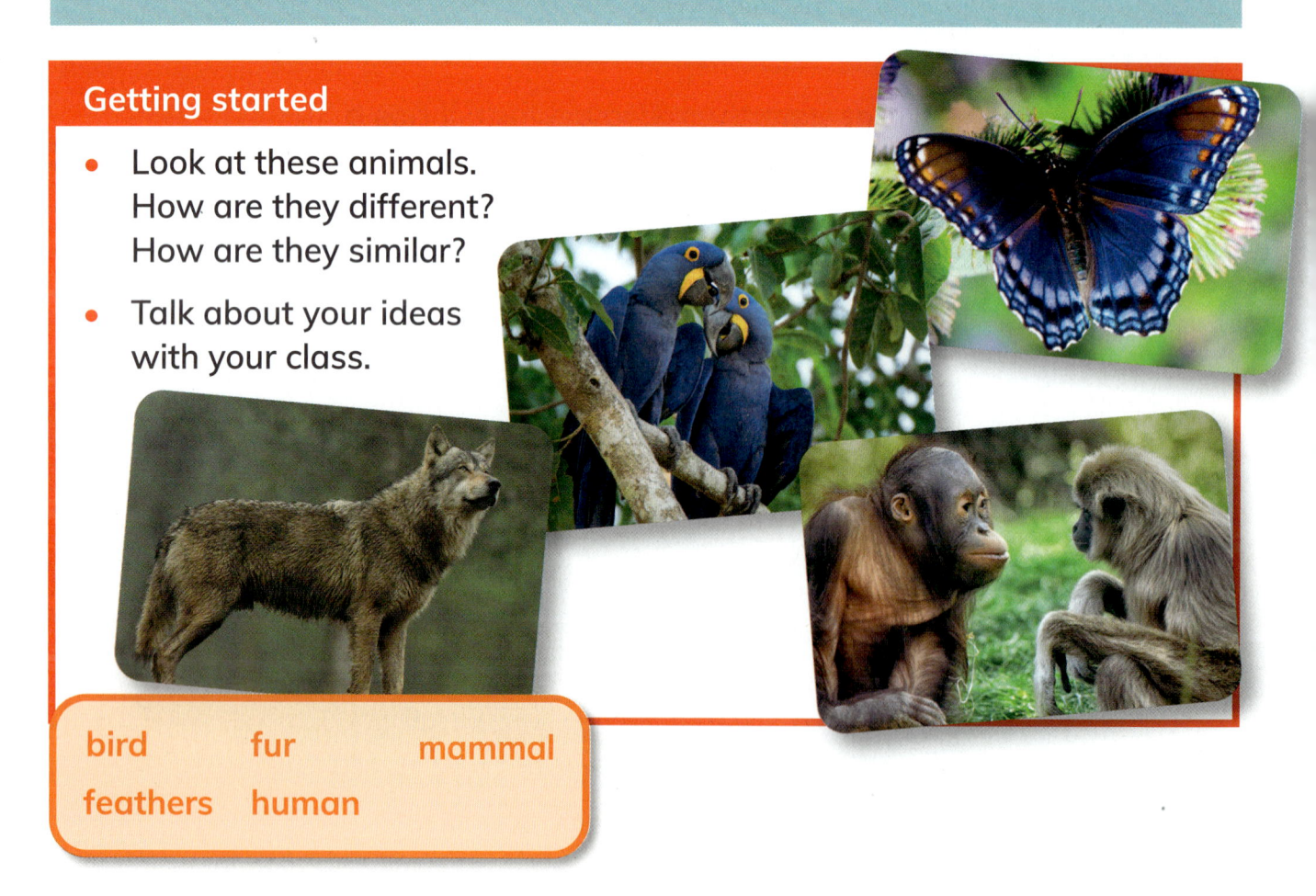

Getting started

- Look at these animals. How are they different? How are they similar?
- Talk about your ideas with your class.

bird   fur   mammal
feathers   human

4.1 Comparing animals

Compare these animals.

The giraffe looks different from the zebra because it has a longer neck.

The giraffe looks similar to the zebra because they both have four legs and a tail.

Giraffes and zebras both have **fur**. Fur is similar to hair.

Animals that have hair or fur are called **mammals**.

People are a special kind of mammal.
We are called **humans**.

Zebra fur

Giraffe fur

Human hair

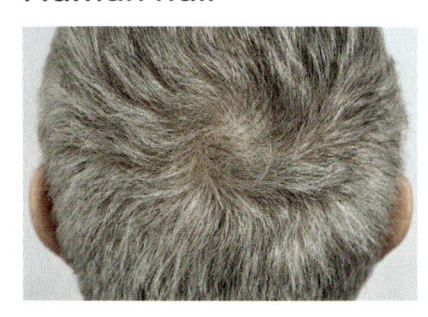

4 Humans and animals grow

Birds look different to mammals. They do not have fur or hair.

Birds have **feathers**.

A bird looks different from a human in many other ways.

A bird looks similar to a human because they both have two legs.

Questions

1. Find another way the giraffe looks different from the zebra.

2. Find two other ways the giraffe and zebra look similar.

3. How does a bird look different from a human?
   Think of as many ways as you can.

4.1 Comparing animals

Think like a scientist 1

Asking questions about animals

You will need:
some books about animals and a computer

Marcus has a question about animals.
How can Marcus find out the answer?

Marcus does not have a real elephant to observe so he uses a book, a video or the internet.

He finds out that elephants do have hair.

Elephants are mammals like humans.

Write your own questions about animals.

Use a book, a video or the internet to find the answers.

Do elephants have hair?

Observing small animals

Sofia has another question about animals.
How can Sofia find out the answer?

How many legs do very small animals have?

4 Humans and animals grow

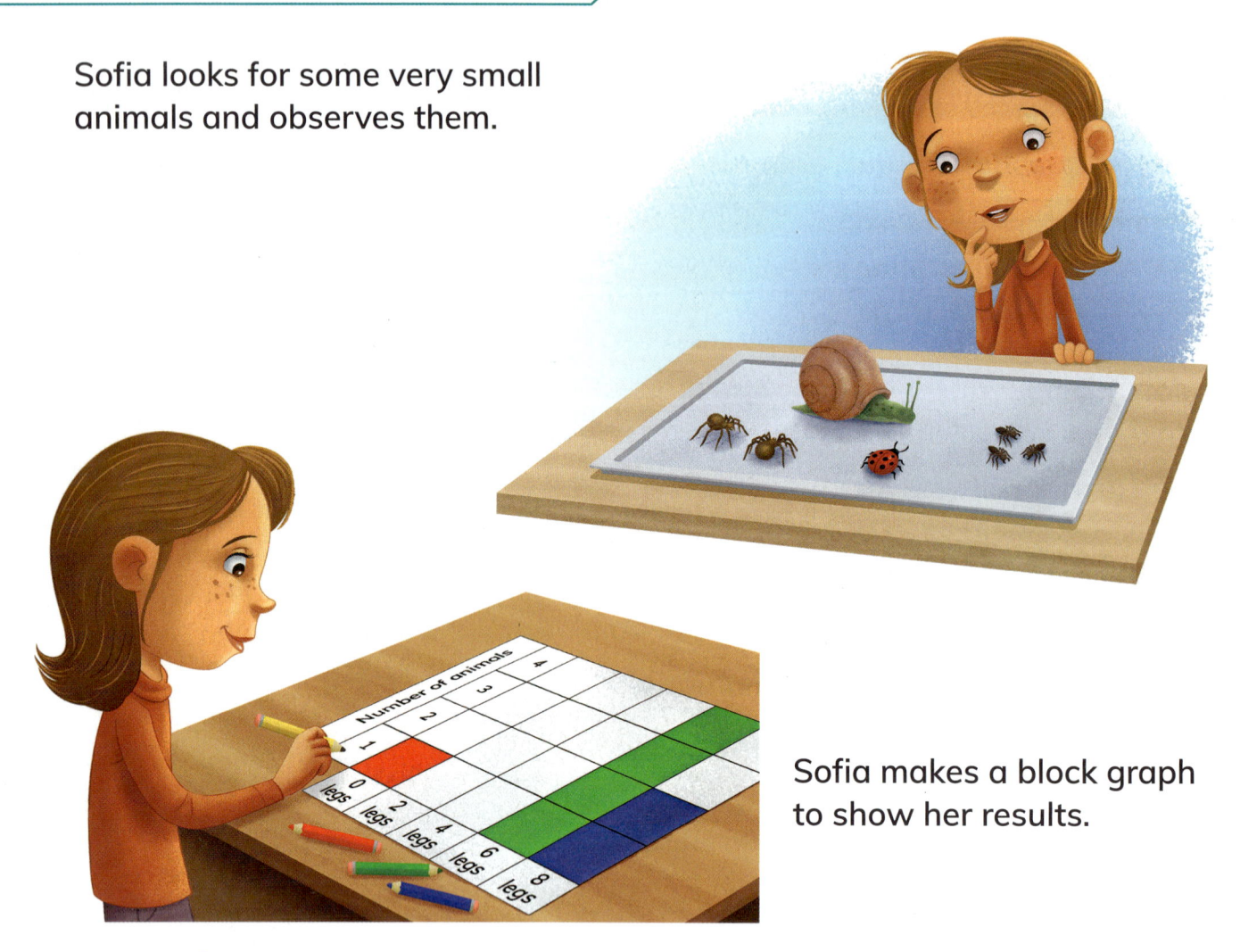

Sofia looks for some very small animals and observes them.

Sofia makes a block graph to show her results.

Questions

4 How many animals did Sofia find with no legs?

5 How many animals did she find with 6 legs?

6 How many animals did she find in total?

Think like a scientist 2

How many legs?

You will need:
a magnifying glass

4.1 Comparing animals

> **Continued**
>
> Find an outdoor habitat in your school.
>
> Observe the small animals that live there.
> Use a magnifying glass to make them easier to see.
>
> How many legs do they have?
>
> **Do not touch animals that can sting or bite.**
>
> Make your own block graph to show your results.
>
> **How am I doing?**
>
> Look at one of the small animals with a friend.
> If you count a different number of legs, count again to check.

Asking questions is an important part of being a scientist.
Do you ask questions about the world?
Does asking questions help you to learn?
You could ask a question that helps people find out something new.

Are there any animals with 5 legs?

Look what I can do!

- [ ] I can say how animals look similar and different.
- [ ] I can ask my own questions about animals.
- [ ] I can use a book, video or the internet to answer questions.
- [ ] I can use and make a block graph.

4 Humans and animals grow

> 4.2 Growing

We are going to:

- learn how humans and other animals change as they grow
- measure how tall we are using bottles
- draw block graphs
- find patterns in results.

Getting started

- How many types of baby animal can you see?
- Do the babies look similar to their parents?
- Which baby animals look similar to their parents? Tell a friend.
- Now say which baby animals look different to their parents.

"Look at the little bear cub"

4.2 Growing

Adults and babies

All animals make babies. The babies are called the animals' **young**.

The young change as they grow **older**. This is called **growth**.

When they are fully grown, we call the animals **adults**.

The young of many animals look similar to the adults.

But the young of some animals look different from the adults.

A young elephant is called a **calf**.

When it gets older it will grow bigger.

adult	growth/grow
age	old/older
baby	parent
calf	pictogram
chick	young
cub	

4 Humans and animals grow

A young penguin is called a **chick**.

When it gets older it will grow different coloured feathers.

Questions

1. The calf looks very similar to the adult elephant. How is it different?
2. The chick looks very different from the adults. How is it similar?

Activity 1

How do baby animals change?

Marcus has a picture of a bear and a baby bear. We call a baby bear a **cub**. He adds notes to the picture to show how the cub changes as it grows.

Look at some pictures of baby animals and adult animals to see how baby animals change as they grow.

Find or draw a picture of an animal and its young.

Make notes to show how the baby animal changes as it grows.

Adult bear
Bear cub
The bear cub grows bigger, gets stronger.

4.2 Growing

Here is a human baby.

Question

3   How do humans change as they grow?

Activity 2

A younger you

Sofia has found a photo taken when she was a baby.

Look at a photo of yourself when you were younger. What did you look like then?

How old are you now? This is called your **age**.

Compare the photo of yourself when you were younger with how you look now. Talk about how you have changed.

4 Humans and animals grow

How humans grow

These pictures show how humans change as they grow older.

baby   toddler   child   teenager   adult   old age

Question

4   Which picture shows people the same age as you?

Sofia uses bottles to measure the height of some people of different ages.

4.2 Growing

She makes a **pictogram** to show the results.

A pictogram is like a block graph but uses pictures instead of blocks.

Look at the ages and the number of bottles. What is the pattern?

Questions

5 How many bottles tall was the child aged 10?

6 How many bottles tall was the adult aged 30?

7 Describe the pattern in the results.

4 Humans and animals grow

Think like a scientist

Measuring height

> **You will need:**
> two identical plastic bottles, a younger child and an adult

Use plastic bottles to measure yourself, a younger child and an adult.

Make a block graph to show your results.

How am I doing?

Ask a friend to check your measuring.

Have you counted the right number of bottles?

Look what I can do!

- ☐ I can describe how humans and some animals change as they grow.
- ☐ I can measure how tall a person is using bottles.
- ☐ I can draw a block graph.
- ☐ I can find patterns in results.

> 4.3 Inheriting characteristics

We are going to:
- find out why animals look similar to their parents
- put children into groups using characteristics.

Getting started
- These animals are all sheep. They all look different.
- Why do you think they look different? Tell a friend what you think.

fingerprint
identical
inherit
stripes
twins

4 Humans and animals grow

The sheep look different because they have different characteristics.

Some have long wool. Some have short wool.

Some have black faces. Some have white faces.

The sheep are different colours.

The sheep have different characteristics because they have different parents. All animals get some of their characteristics from their parents.

We say that animals **inherit** characteristics from their parents.

Animals look similar to their parents but they do not look the same. We say they are not **identical**. This is because an animal inherits some characteristics from one parent and some characteristics from the other parent.

Every tiger has a different pattern of **stripes**.

A tiger cub's stripes are not the same as its parents' stripes, but they are similar.

4.3 Inheriting characteristics

This is a human **fingerprint**.

Every person has a different pattern in their fingerprint.

Your fingerprints are not the same as your parents' fingerprints, but they are similar.

There are many other characteristics we inherit from our parents.

Usually they make us look different from each other.

These children are identical **twins**. They look the same because they have inherited the same characteristics from their parents.

Activity

How are you different?

Here are five characteristics.

Which characteristics do you have? Look in a mirror.

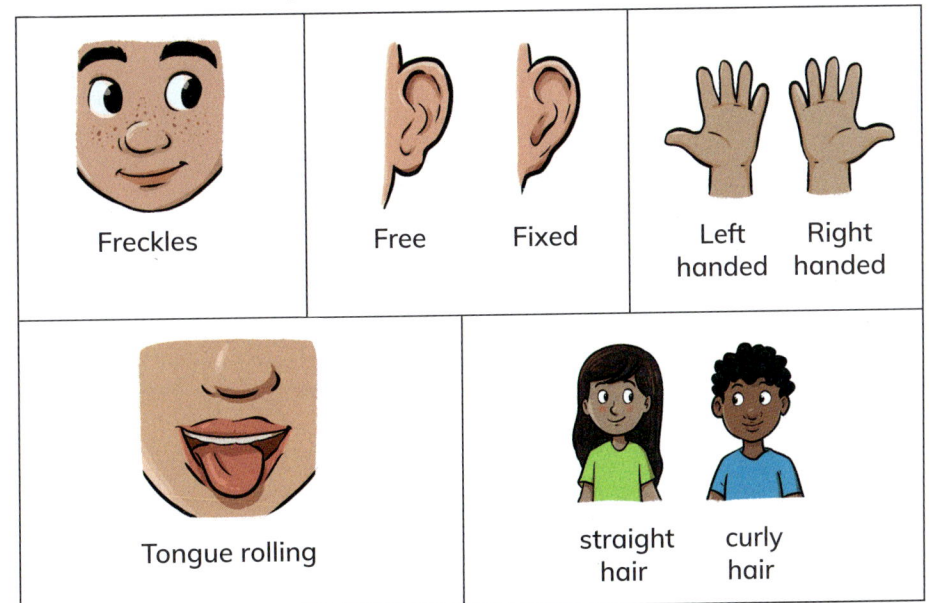

- Freckles
- Free / Fixed
- Left handed / Right handed
- Tongue rolling
- straight hair / curly hair

103

4 Humans and animals grow

Continued

Talk to your friends.

Make groups of children with similar characteristics.

Does anyone have all the same characteristics as you?

Think like a scientist

Sorting fingerprints

You will need:
a balloon and a marker pen

Observe your fingerprints to find out which type of fingerprint you have.

Look at the pictures to see what to do.

4.3 Inheriting characteristics

Continued

Compare your fingerprint with these three pictures.
Which types of fingerprint do you have?

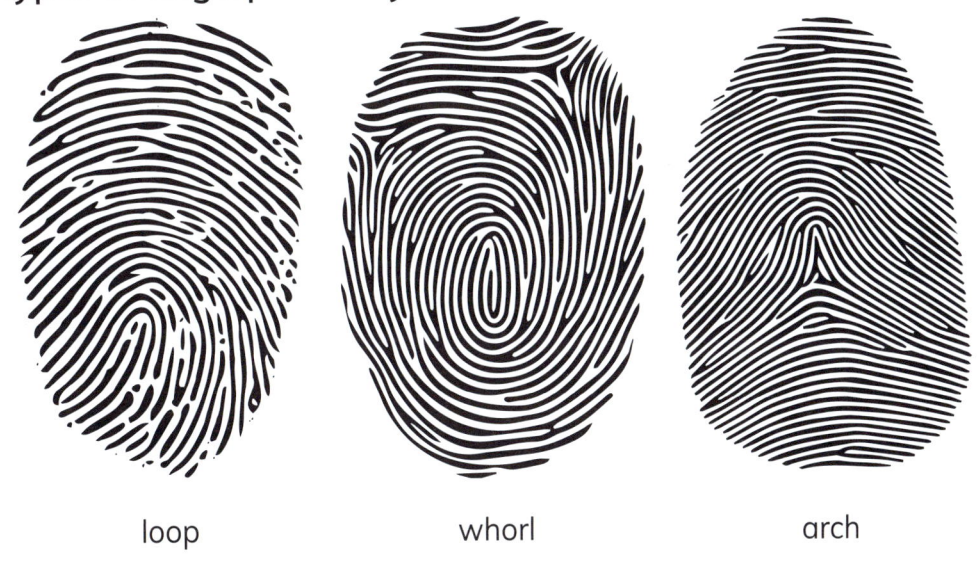

loop　　　　　　　whorl　　　　　　　arch

How am I doing?

Have a look at your friends' fingerprints. Which types do they have?

Have they sorted their fingerprint correctly?

Fingerprint patterns are difficult to see. You used a balloon to make them larger. Can you think of a different way of looking at fingerprints? What could you use to make fingerprints look larger?

Look what I can do!

☐　I can explain why animals look similar to their parents.

☐　I can put children into groups using characteristics.

4 Humans and animals grow

> 4.4 Keeping healthy

We are going to:
- find out how to keep healthy
- find out why humans get ill and what it does to our bodies
- sort food into groups
- say if our predictions are correct or not.

Getting started
- Bimla wants to eat food that is good for her. What should she eat?

Eat chocolate. Sugar gives you energy.

Eat food that tastes good.

Drink milk. It makes you strong.

Fruit and vegetables are good for you.

clean	germs	ill	sick
diet	headache	illness	sweat
exercise	heart	muscles	

Healthy eating

Food that is good for us is called healthy food. Humans need to eat lots of different foods to stay healthy. The food we eat is called our **diet**.

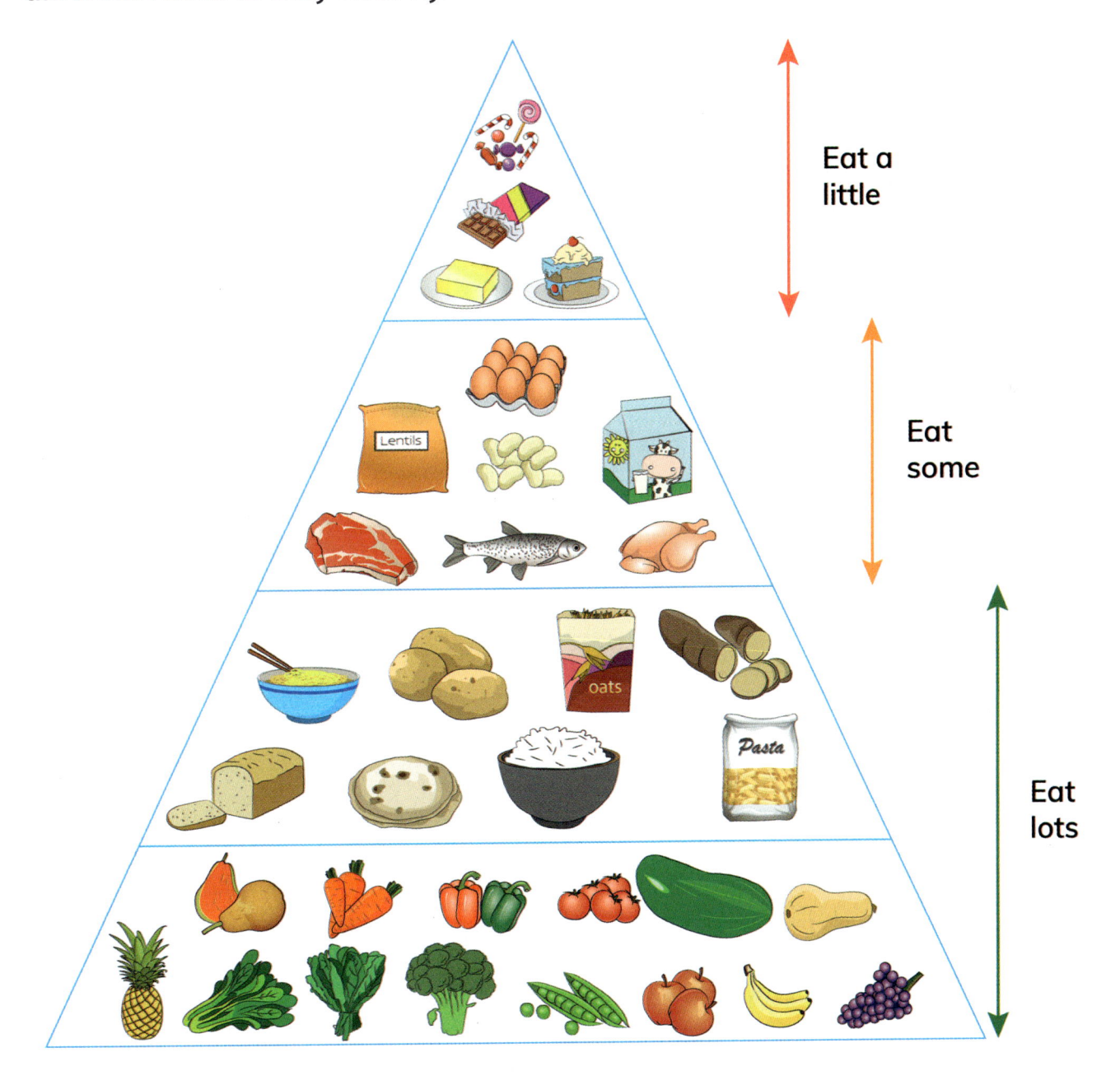

Eat a little

Eat some

Eat lots

This food triangle shows how much of each type of food we should eat.

If we do not have a healthy diet our bodies might not get what they need.

This is one way we can become **ill**.

4 Humans and animals grow

Activity

Sorting food

Marcus and Zara are sorting food into groups.

Try doing this with some foods or pictures of foods. Look at the food triangle to work out where to put each food.

Being ill

Nobody feels good all the time. When we feel **sick** or have a **headache** we say we are ill or we have an **illness**.

Germs are living things that are too small to see. Some germs can make us ill. This happens when the germs get inside us and our bodies cannot kill them. This is another way we can become ill.

4.4 Keeping healthy

Do these things to stop germs getting into your body.

Wash your hands after going to the toilet.

Wash your hands before eating.

Do not eat dirty food or drink dirty water.

Sometimes germs can make us cough or sneeze.

Cover your mouth when you cough or sneeze.

This can stop germs getting to other people.

Healthy people become ill less often. Their bodies are better at killing germs.

Question

1 Have you had an illness? How did you feel?

4 Humans and animals grow

Exercise and keeping clean

We can also make our bodies healthy by doing **exercise**. Exercise is when we use our **muscles** to move our bodies. It makes our muscles stronger.

Humans should do some exercise most days.

Your **heart** is a muscle.

Exercise is good for your heart.

Exercising makes us **sweat**.

We need to wash after exercising to keep **clean**.

Keeping clean is another way to keep your body healthy.

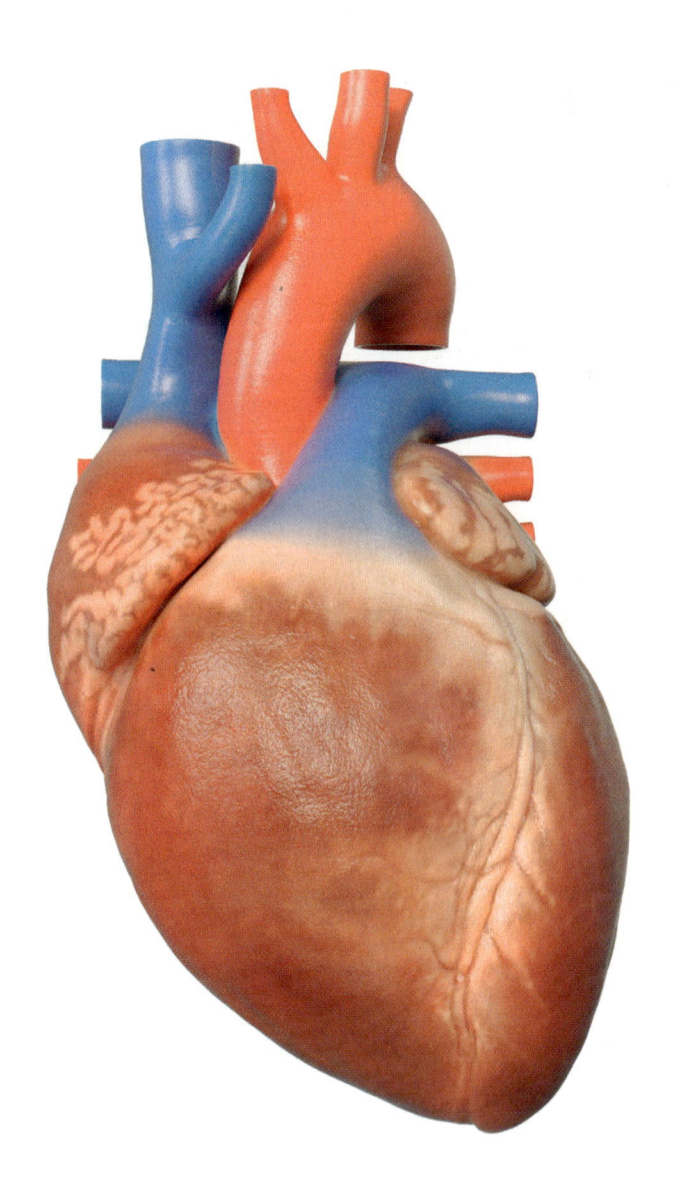

Questions

2 Which of these is exercise?

running   reading   swimming

playing football   sleeping

3 Which parts of the body get stronger when you exercise?

4 Why is it good to wash your hands before eating?

4.4 Keeping healthy

Think like a scientist

What happens when we exercise?

You will need: a timer

Heart. How fast?

Skin. Cool or warm?

Skin. Cool or warm?

Heart. How fast?

at rest — do some exercise — after exercise

Breathing. How fast?

Breathing. How fast?

Look at the pictures to see what to do.

Tell a friend what you think will happen.

Think about your breathing, your heart and your skin.

Were your predictions correct? Did you observe any other changes?

How am I doing?

Were your friend's predictions correct?

Tell them what you think.

Look what I can do!

☐ I can talk about three ways to keep healthy.
☐ I can say why humans get ill and what being ill does to our bodies.
☐ I can sort food into groups.
☐ I can say if my predictions are correct or not.

4 Humans and animals grow

> 4.5 Teeth

We are going to:
- learn about the different types of teeth and what they do
- learn about how to look after teeth
- say if our predictions are correct or not
- observe human teeth and make models of them
- investigate teeth safely.

Getting started
- Draw some teeth.
- Add labels to show what you know about teeth.

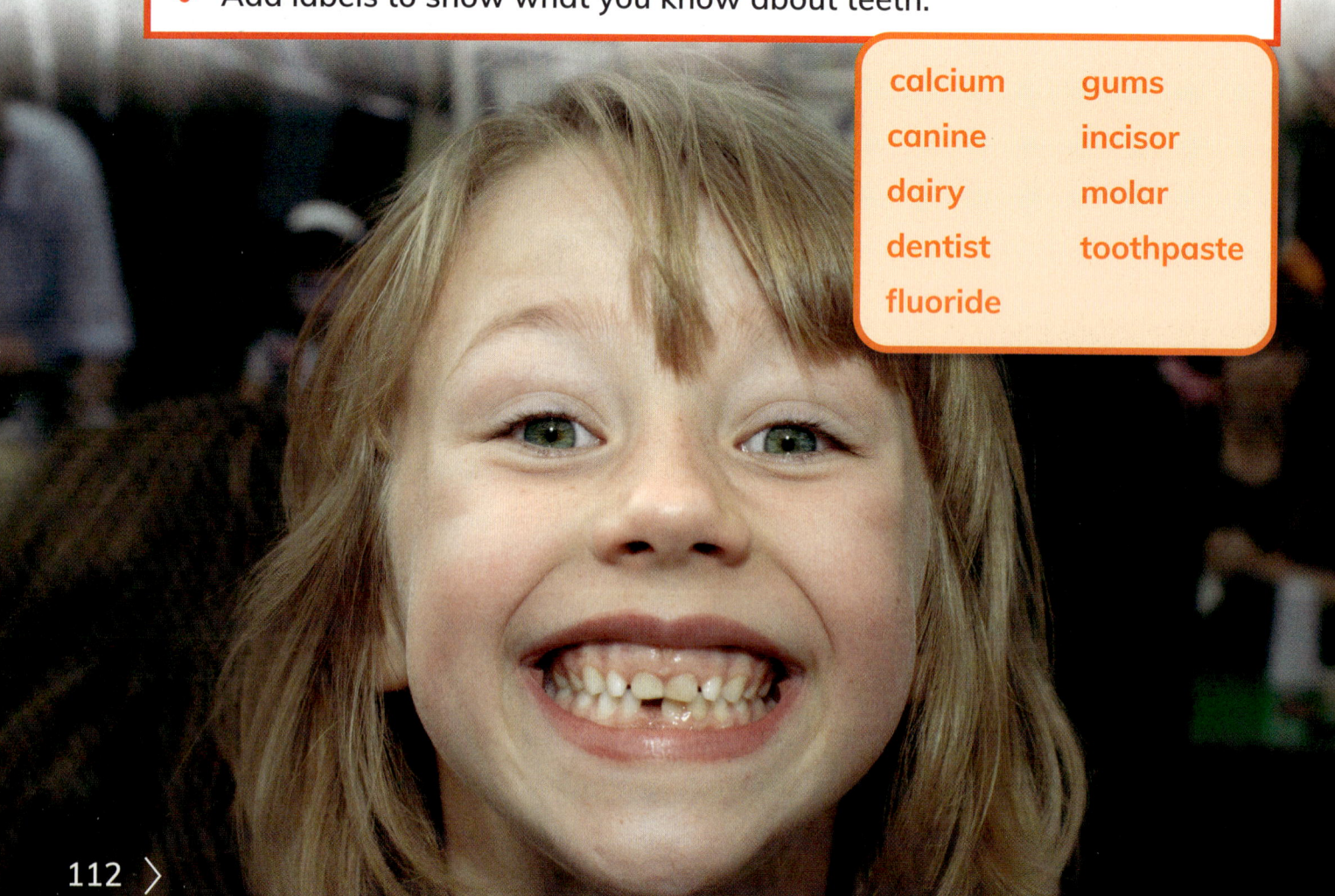

calcium   gums
canine   incisor
dairy   molar
dentist   toothpaste
fluoride

4.5 Teeth

Looking after teeth

We need to look after our teeth.

We use teeth to eat and we also use teeth to talk.

You can keep your teeth healthy by eating a healthy diet. **Calcium** is a material that helps to make teeth strong. Milk and other **dairy** foods, some beans and some fish have calcium in them. Make sure you eat some of these foods.

Food with lots of sugar is bad for teeth. Eat very little food with lots of sugar.

Brush your teeth twice every day for two minutes to keep them clean. Use **toothpaste** with **fluoride** in it. Fluoride helps to make your teeth strong.

Do not use too much toothpaste.

Go to the **dentist** twice a year. The dentist will check your teeth are healthy and can help you look after them.

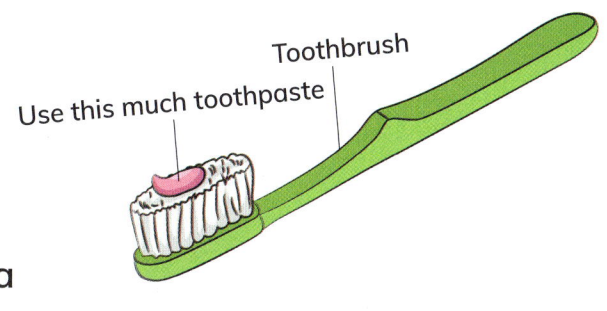

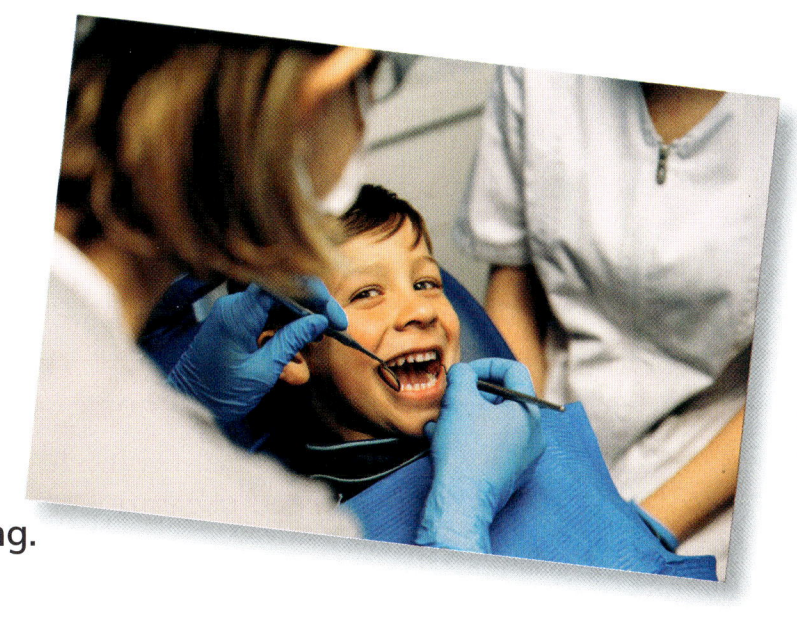

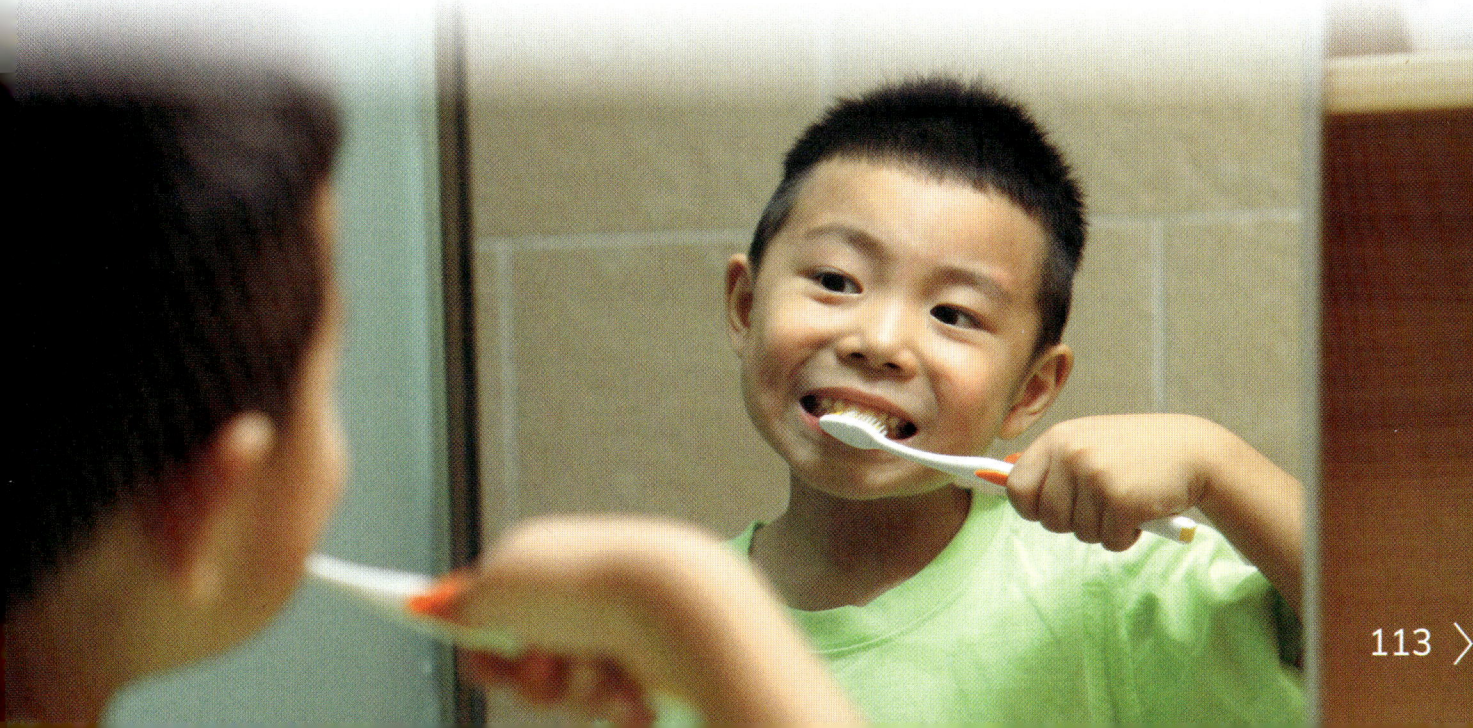

4 Humans and animals grow

Questions

1. What three things can you do to look after your teeth?
2. How much toothpaste should you use?
3. What do calcium and fluoride do?

Think like a scientist 1

What does sugar do to teeth?

You will need:
a drink with lots of sugar, water, egg shells and two cups

Teeth are made of a similar material to egg shells.

To find out what sugar does to our teeth we can investigate what sugar does to egg shells. Look at the pictures to see what to do.

Predict what will happen to the egg shell in each cup.
Record your prediction in a diagram.

| Place half an egg shell into each cup. | Add water to one cup and a sugary drink to the other. | After seven days see what has happened to the egg shell. |

What did you find out at the end?

Explain what too much sugar can do to teeth.

How am I doing?

Look at your predictions.
Can you say which were correct and which were not?

4.5 Teeth

Types of teeth

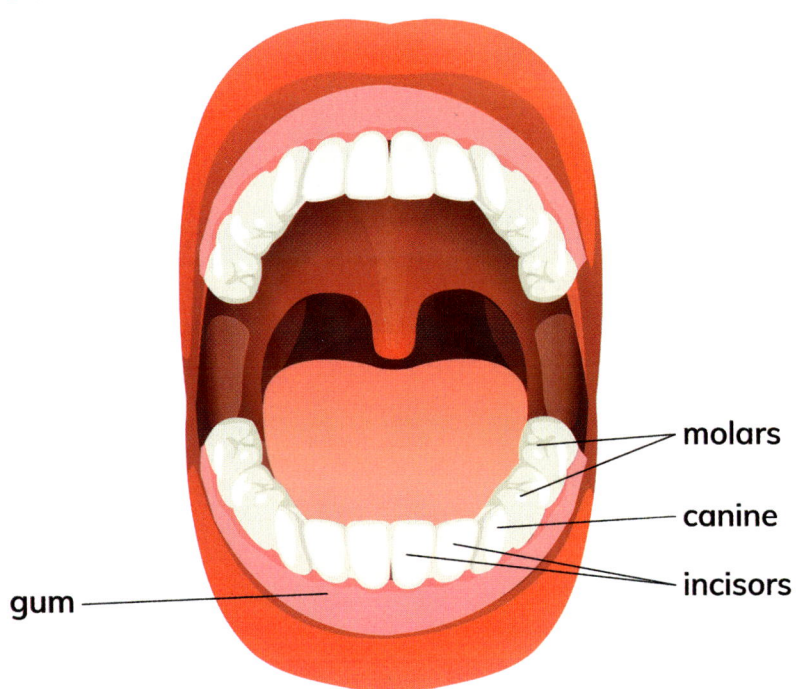

Humans have three main types of teeth: **incisors**, **canines** and **molars**. Teeth have roots to fix them to your **gums**.

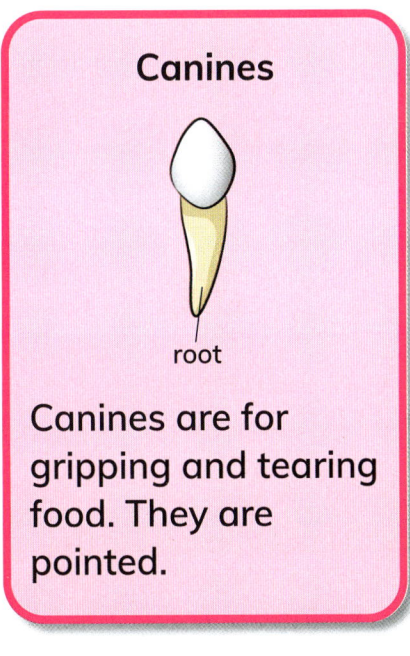

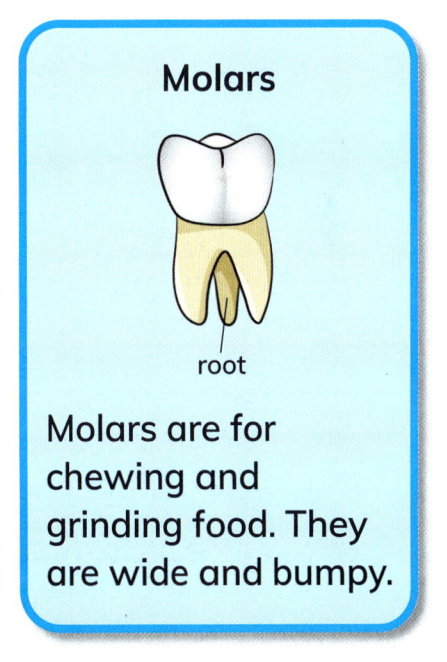

Incisors
Incisors are for biting food. They are straight at the top and sharp.

Canines
Canines are for gripping and tearing food. They are pointed.

Molars
Molars are for chewing and grinding food. They are wide and bumpy.

Children have 20 baby teeth. As you grow older these teeth will fall out because larger adult teeth are growing in your gums. Adults have 32 teeth.

4 Humans and animals grow

Think like a scientist 2

Making model teeth

> **You will need:**
> a mirror and some modelling clay

Marcus is making a model of his teeth.
He is using a mirror to see how they look.

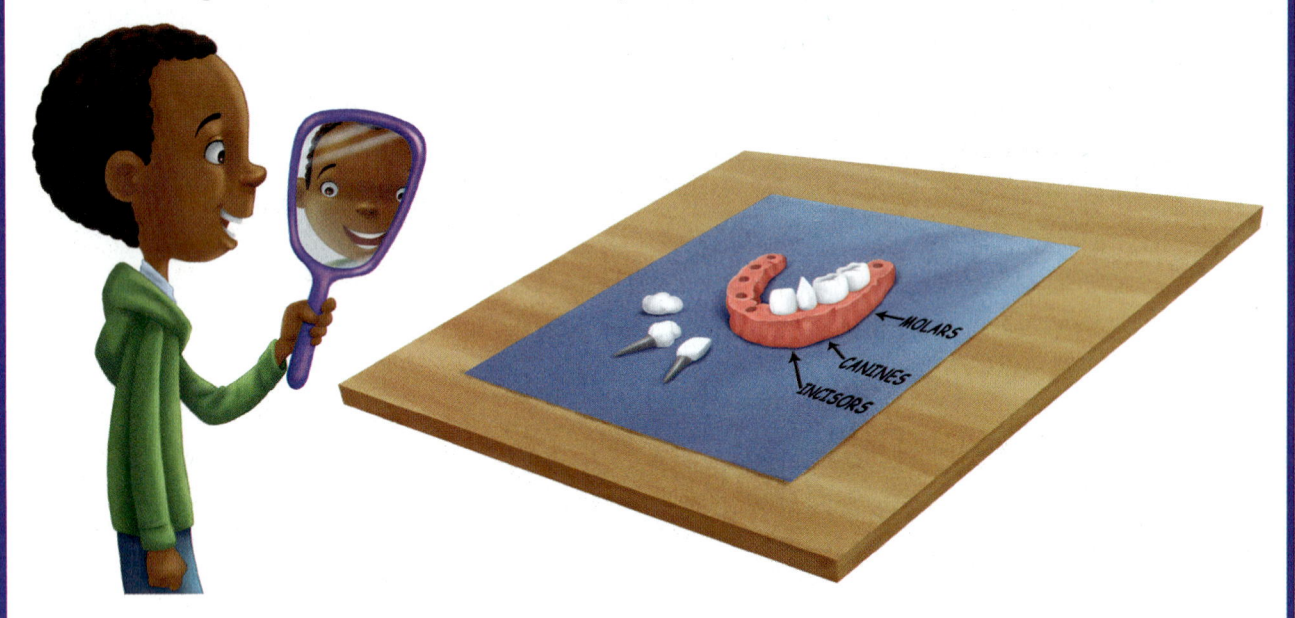

Make a model of your own teeth.

Look at them using a mirror. Touch and feel them too.

**Wash your hands before and after you touch your teeth.
Do not touch other people's teeth.**

Scientists often make and use models.
It is a good way to learn more about something.
What did you learn from making your model teeth?

Project: People who use science

Look what I can do!

- ☐ I can describe the three types of teeth and what they do.
- ☐ I can explain how to look after my teeth.
- ☐ I can say if my predictions are correct or not.
- ☐ I can make model teeth and say how they are like real teeth.
- ☐ I can stay safe when I do an investigation.

Project: People who use science

There are lots of people who use science in their jobs.

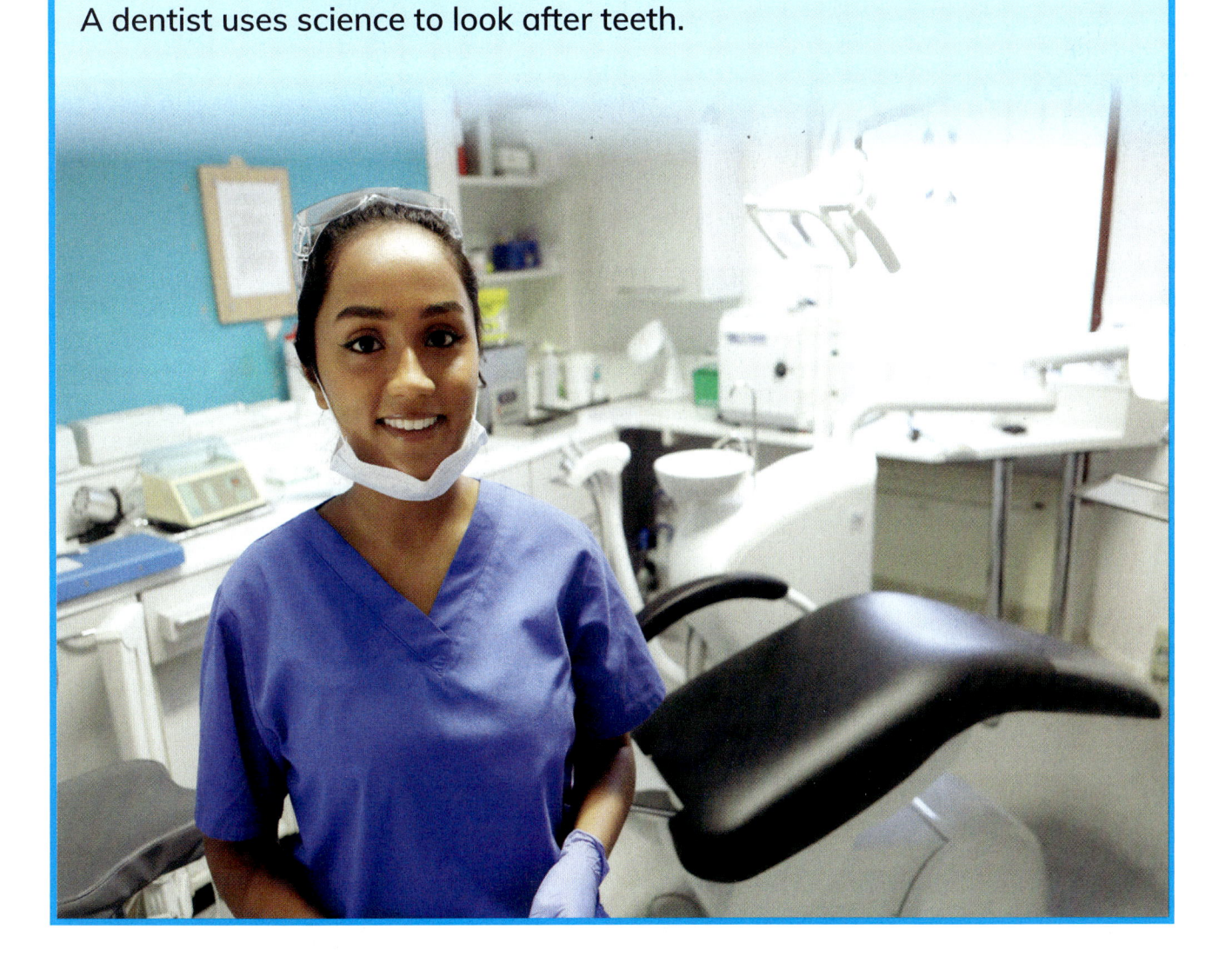

A dentist uses science to look after teeth.

4   Humans and animals grow

Continued

A sports coach uses science to plan the best exercises.

The police use science to catch people who have done things that are wrong.

Project: People who use science

Continued

A zoologist uses science to learn about animals.

Make a poster about a job that uses science.

You could use books or the internet to find out about one of the jobs shown here.

You could find out about a different job.

Maybe an adult you know uses science in their job.

4 Humans and animals grow

Check your progress

Talk about the answers to these questions with your class.

1. How do this newt and this fish look similar?
   How do they look different?

2. Find the adult animals and their young.

Check your progress

Continued

3 Which of these foods are healthy?

4 Which of these is exercise?

4 Humans and animals grow

Continued

5 What three things can Zara do to look after her teeth?

5 Light

> 5.1 Light sources

We are going to:

- find different light sources, including the Sun
- record observations on a table
- sort objects into groups
- find light sources powered by electricity.

Getting started

- Have you seen fireworks at night? Fireworks burn very brightly. They are a **light source**.
- Ask your friend to point to other light sources in the picture. Are they right?
- Think of a light source that gives us light during the day.

bright   Moon
flashlight   reflect
light source   shine

5 Light

A light source makes light.

At night, street lights give us light.

In the day time, we get most of our light from the Sun.

Never look at the Sun as it will hurt your eyes.

Light sources can be flames, electric lights, TVs and computer screens. The light from a light source shines onto things which we can then see.

Some materials reflect light, they do not make light. They reflect light from a light source such as a flashlight

The things in these pictures are not light sources.

The Moon reflects light from the Sun.

Glass reflects light.

Materials which reflect a lot of light look bright.

5.1 Light sources

The sea reflects light.

Question

1. Make a list of all the different light sources in this picture.

125

5 Light

Activity 1

Is it a light source?

Look at these objects.

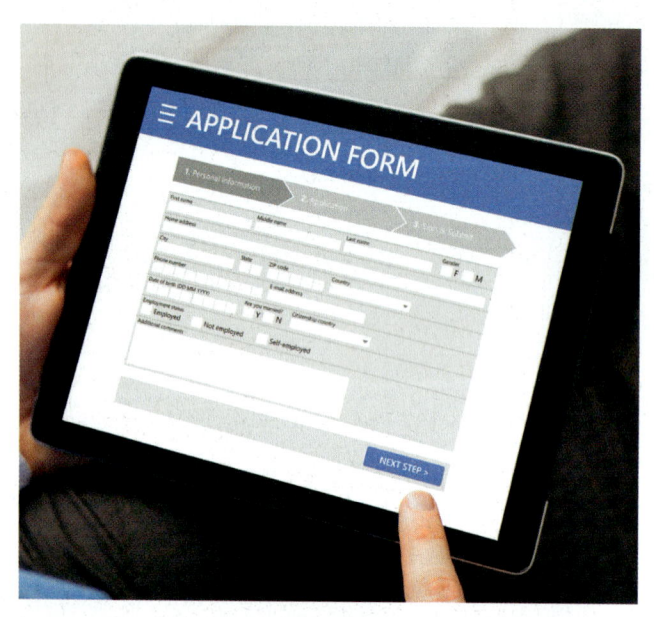

Put the objects into two groups, 'light sources' and 'not light sources'.

5.1 Light sources

Activity 2

So many light sources

Look at objects around your school.

Ask the question, is this a light source?

Record your answer in a table like this.

object	Is it a light source?	
	yes	no
door		no

Find light sources powered by electricity.

Are most light sources in school powered by electricity?

Why is this?

We have many light sources. Some are brighter than others.

Question

2   Look at these light sources.
    Which is brightest?
    Which is least bright?

127

5 Light

Think like a scientist

Which flashlight is brighter?

You will need:
three different flashlights, sheets of paper

Some flashlights are brighter than other flashlights.

Use this test to see which flashlight is brightest.

Remember, never look at very bright lights. They can hurt your eyes.

Hold sheets of paper to stop the light from the flashlight.

Then count how many sheets are needed to stop the light.

Record your results on a table like this.

Flashlight	Number of sheets needed to stop the light
small red flashlight	4

After the test, show your friends what you did.

Which flashlight was the brightest?

Why are some flashlights brighter than others?

5.1 Light sources

> **Continued**
>
> **How am I doing?**
>
> On one side of a piece of paper, draw a light source which is not powered by electricity. On the other side of the paper, draw a light source powered by electricity. Ask a friend to show you one of their pictures. Now match it with yours. Is it powered by electricity or not?

When you record your results, how does this help you learn?

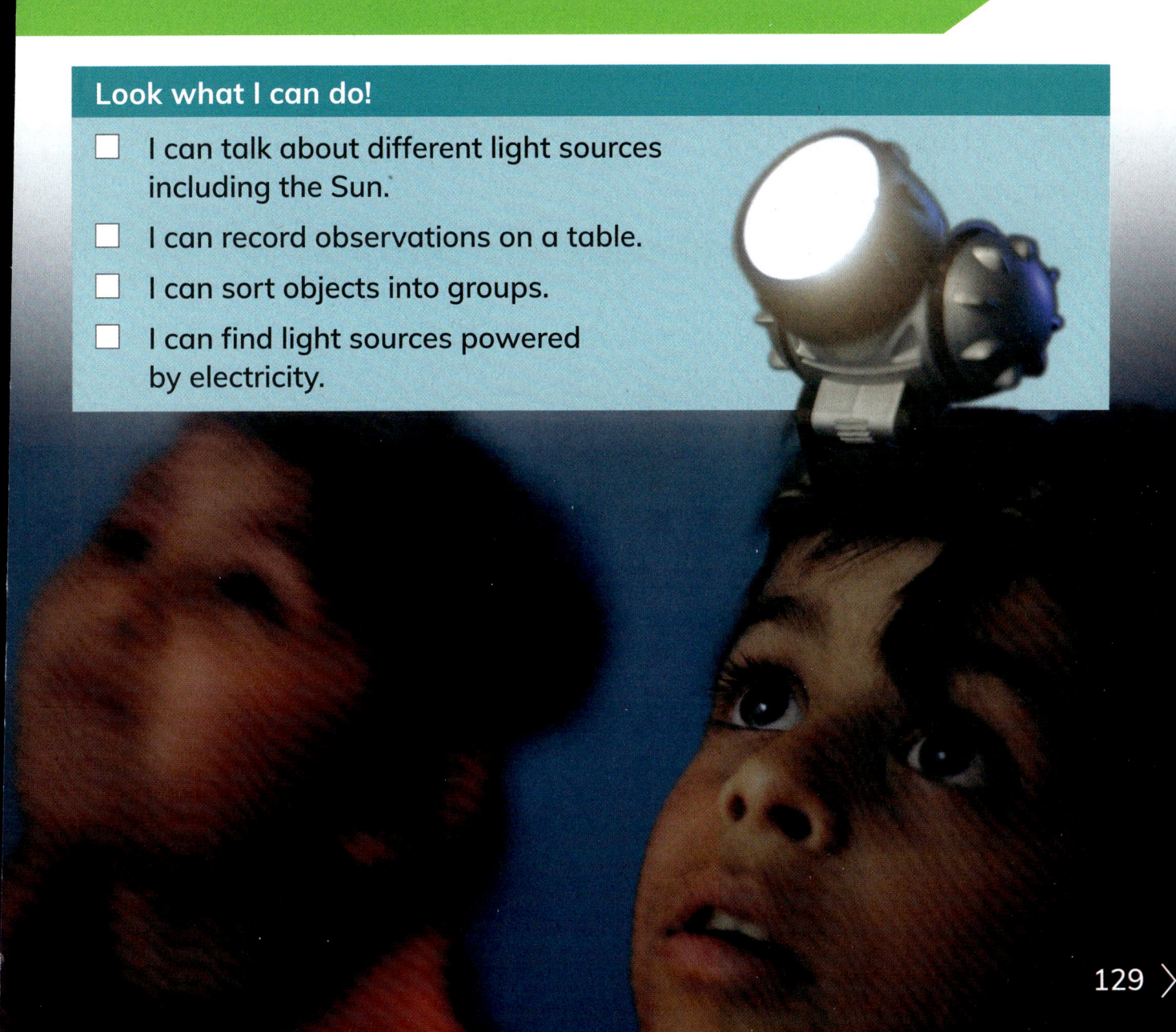

Look what I can do!

☐ I can talk about different light sources including the Sun.

☐ I can record observations on a table.

☐ I can sort objects into groups.

☐ I can find light sources powered by electricity.

5 Light

> 5.2 Darkness

We are going to:

- learn that with little or no light there is darkness
- record observations on a table
- find patterns in results.

Getting started

- Why is there light in this cave?
  What would it be like without the light?

- What is the darkest place you have ever been? What was it like?
  Write down three words to describe it.

5.2 Darkness

Hafeez is in his bedroom, it is **night time**.
It is **dark** in his room but there is some light.

> dark
> night time

I can see in the dark!

Questions

1 Where is the light getting in?
2 Where is the light coming from?

If there is no light from a light source, it will be too dark to see.
We need some light to see things.

At night we don't have sunlight, so we use light sources to make light.

These children are making a dark place in their classroom.

5 Light

Questions

3 What are the four objects they have put in the dark?

4 Can you see the white object?

5 Can you see the coloured objects?

6 Are some colours easier to see in the dark?

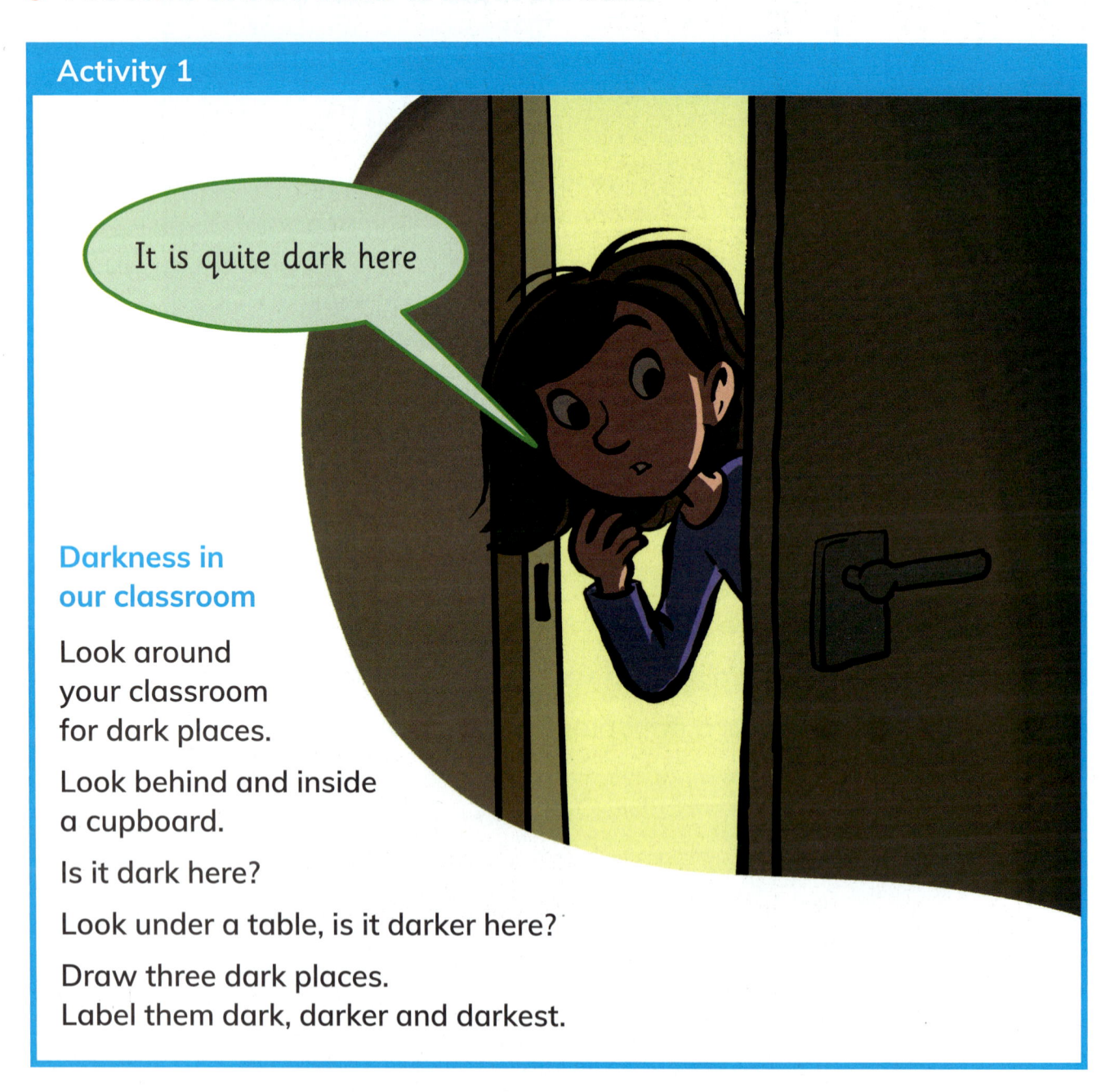

Activity 1

It is quite dark here

Darkness in our classroom

Look around your classroom for dark places.

Look behind and inside a cupboard.

Is it dark here?

Look under a table, is it darker here?

Draw three dark places.
Label them dark, darker and darkest.

5.2 Darkness

Activity 2

Using a dark box

You will need:
a box with a small hole in the side, different coloured objects

We can do a test by putting objects in a dark box.

Put a dark-coloured object into a box like this.
Put the lid on and look through the hole. Can you see the object?

Finish this sentence.

It is hard to see the _____ in the box because _____.

Now try this investigation with a light-coloured object.
Are the results the same?

5 Light

Working in the dark

Some people work underground.
They have bright lights so they can see.
They have clothes which reflect light so they can be seen.

Some people work at night.
They also need bright lights and clothes which reflect light.

Think like a scientist

How much light do I need to see?

You will need:
a box with a hole in the side and a flap in the top,
small coloured objects

Continued

Now use a box with a flap in the top.

Put an object in the box. Predict whether it will be easy or hard to see. Then observe the object with the flap closed, open a little and then open. Record what you see on a table like this.

Do the same with the other objects.

object	colour	lid closed	lid open a little	lid wide open
brick	red	hard to see	I can see	easy to see the brick

Which colours are easier to see?

Why are they easier to see?

Were your predictions right?

Is there a pattern in the results?

5 Light

> **Continued**
>
> **How am I doing?**
>
> During the daytime, where would you find a dark place?
> Put one finger up for every place you can say. Now tell your friend.

When you learn science at school, do you think about it after school? Does this help you learn?

Look what I can do!

- ☐ I can say that without light it is dark.
- ☐ I can record observations on a table.
- ☐ I can find patterns in results.

> 5.3 The Sun appears to move!

We are going to:

- investigate how the Sun seems to move during the day
- talk about the difference between a diagram and a picture
- draw and label a diagram
- look for patterns in results.

Getting started

- Look at this picture, it is the end of the day. Can you describe what this will look like in an hour?

daylight   star
position   sundial

5 Light

The Sun appears to move.

The position of the Sun changes during the day.

Early today the Sun appeared low down.

Our nearest **star** is the Sun. It is very bright and hot.

During the hours of **daylight**, the Sun gives us light.

The Sun is a very big light source.

The Sun looks as though it moves across the sky.

Questions

1. Do you agree with these children?
2. Can you describe the way the Sun appears to move each day?

5.3 The Sun appears to move!

This diagram shows the Sun at 4 o'clock in the afternoon.

Look at how the Sun's position in the sky has changed during the day.

Point to the place that the Sun would appear at 3 o'clock in the afternoon.

midday

10 o'clock in the morning

2 o'clock in the afternoon

8 o'clock in the morning

4 o'clock in the afternoon

Activity

Looking at patterns

Go outside to a place where you can see a lot of the sky.

Find the Sun in the sky but do not look straight at it.

Never look at the Sun, it will damage your eyes.

139

5 Light

> **Continued**
>
> Draw a diagram like this one to show where the Sun is early in the morning. Write down the time on your diagram.
>
> A diagram is better than a picture because a diagram has extra information.
>
> Add the **position** of the Sun to the diagram at different times of the day.
>
> 12.00 noon
> 11.00 am
> 10.00 am
> 9.00 am
>
> Look for a pattern in what you recorded.
>
> Does the Sun's position appear to change? How?
>
> When is the Sun highest in the sky?

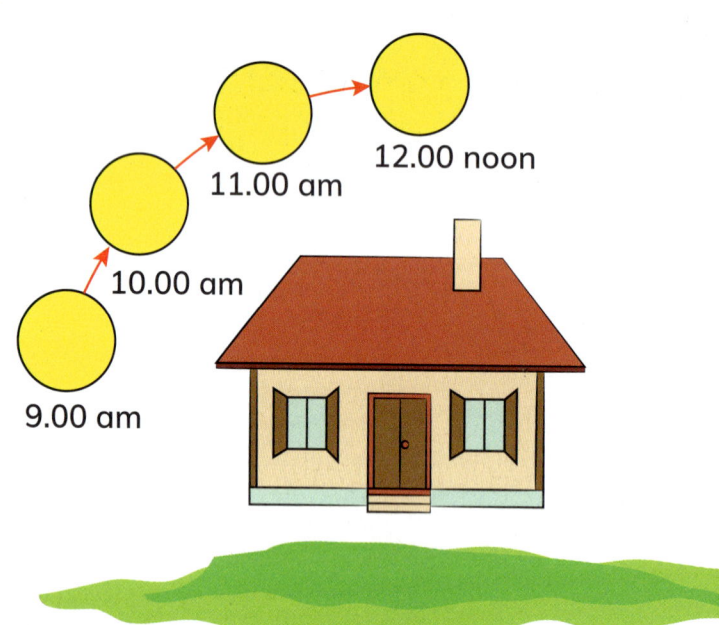

5.3 The Sun appears to move!

Think like a scientist

Showing the way the Sun appears to move!

You will need:
card, coloured crayons, a magnet, a paper clip, sticky tape.

The children wanted to make a model showing how the Sun appears to move across the sky.

They stuck a paper model of the Sun onto a metal paper clip.

Then they could move the model Sun using a magnet from behind a card.

Can you make this model?

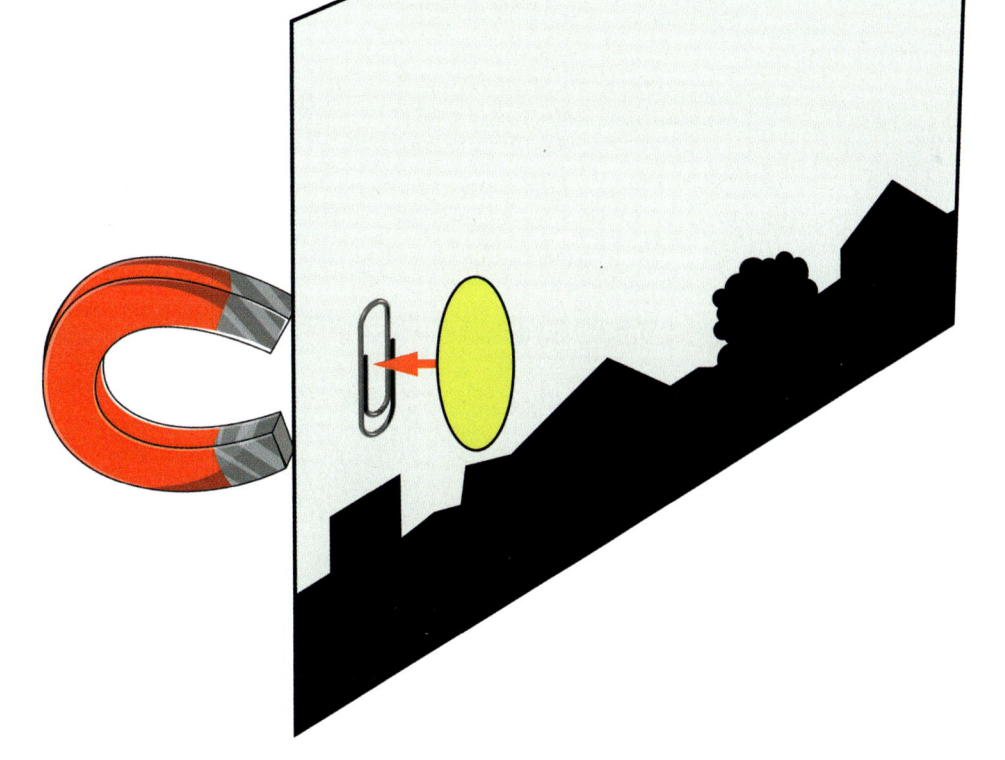

Can you show how the Sun appears to move in the sky?

5 Light

In this topic we use pictures and a diagram. A diagram has extra information on it. How does this help us to learn science?

Look what I can do!

- ☐ I can investigate the way the Sun seems to move in the day.
- ☐ I can talk about the difference between a diagram and a picture.
- ☐ I can draw and label a diagram.
- ☐ I can see patterns in results.

Project: My book of light

Long ago, people did not understand light. Some thought it was a kind of air.

Just over 300 years ago, Isaac Newton wrote a book about light. He asked questions such as 'What is light?'. We still use some of his ideas today, but now we understand much more about light.

Isaac Newton and other people did experiments to find out about light.

Find more information about Isaac Newton. Look in science books and on the internet. Make notes and share these with your friends.

Now write about light or make a poster about light.

You can write about:

- Isaac Newton (don't forget that his ideas were new at the time)
- light sources
- things that are not light sources
- darkness
- ways we use light
- some of our activities in this topic.

5 Light

Check your progress

Talk about the answers to these questions with your class.

1 Which of these is a light source?

A
B
C
D
E

2 Drisha has lost her ball.

   a Why can't she find it?

   b What could she use to help find the ball?

Continued

3 Which light sources are powered by electricity?

A B C D

4 Where would the Sun appear to be at 1pm?

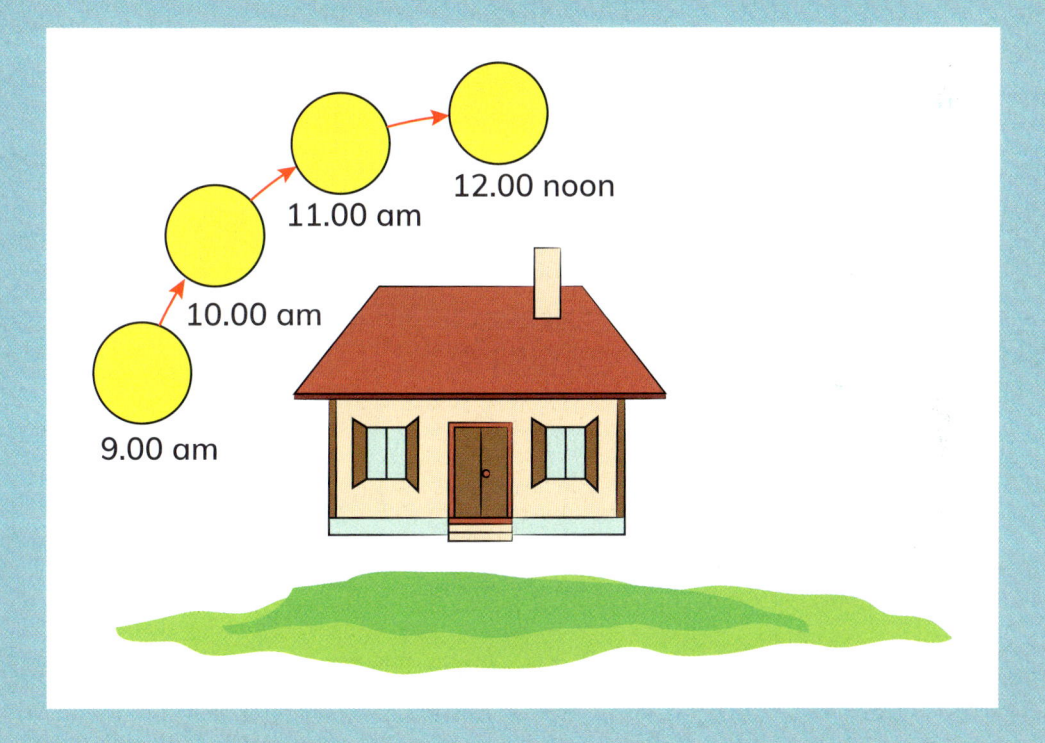

9.00 am → 10.00 am → 11.00 am → 12.00 noon

6 Electricity

> 6.1 Where do we use electricity?

We are going to:
- investigate the different ways we use electricity
- sort and group different types of switches
- find the answer to questions by using books and the internet.

Getting started

- This is the Mars Curiosity Rover. It is a **robot** on planet Mars. It is looking for water on Mars. The robot uses **electricity** to move, test for water, look for rocks and take photographs.

- The robot moves on its wheels and has arms it can move.

- Try to think of other **electrical appliances** which move.

cell
dangerous
discovery
electrical appliance
electricity
invention
mains electricity
plug
power station
robot
rocked
slide
switch
wire

6.1 Where do we use electricity?

We use electricity to do lots of things.

Question

1 Look at the picture. How do we use electricity to:

- make light?
- make sound?
- heat things up?
- cool things down?
- make things move?

Look for things in the picture that use **mains electricity**.
We call these things appliances. These things have a **wire** and **plug**.

Only adults should move, plug in and unplug mains electrical appliances. Mains electricity is very powerful. It can be dangerous. It can kill you.

6 Electricity

Mains electricity is made in a **power station**. The electricity travels along the wires, high in the air, so that we are safe. The wires take the electricity to all the places we need it.

A **cell** is a source of electricity. Cells are used to power electrical appliances that people carry around like flashlights, watches or mobile phones.

6.1 Where do we use electricity?

Question

2   Which cell will fit into which electrical appliance? Choose from flashlight, watch and mobile phone.

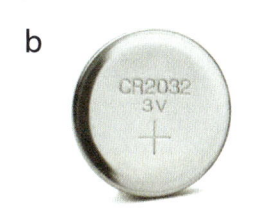

a   b   c

Activity 1

Electricity in school

Look at different things around your school.
Say if you think they are powered by electricity.
How do you know if something is powered by electricity?
Do some of these electrical appliances use cells?
Do some use mains electricity?
What do these electrical appliances do?
Are they safe for children to use?

Switches

Electrical appliances have on/off **switches**.

Look at an appliance in class.
Does it have a switch? How does the switch move?

Did you see switches on the appliances you used today?

Some switches can be pressed, some **slide** and some can be **rocked**.

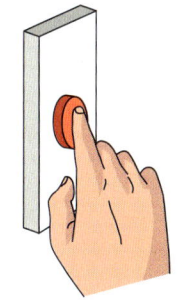

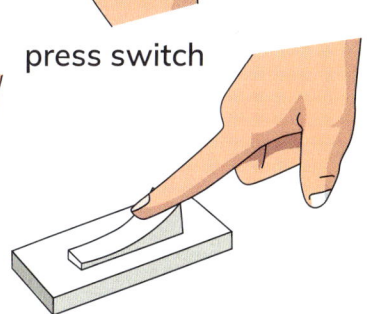

press switch

slide switch   rocker switch

6 Electricity

Activity 2

Which switch?

You will need:
electrical appliances powered by cells

Try to group the different switches.

Name the appliance and draw the switch in a table like this.

Electrical appliances powered by cells		
press switches	rocker switches	slide switches
door bell		

Michael Faraday

Over 200 years ago, Michael Faraday found out many things about electricity.

One **discovery** was that electricity could move things. We now use his science in all the electrical appliances we use today.

Faraday's **inventions** made electricity very useful to us.

6.1 Where do we use electricity?

> **Think like a scientist**
>
> **Finding out about electricity**
>
> > **You will need:**
> > books about electricity, the internet
>
> Use books and the internet to find answers to these questions.
> - What do we use electricity for?
> - What were Thomas Edison's inventions?
> - What were Michael Faraday's discoveries?
>
> Make a poster to show what you have found.
>
> **How am I doing?**
>
> Pretend that your friend is Michael Faraday.
> Tell him about all the things we use his discoveries for.

Thomas Edison was a great inventor. He invented the electric light bulb. When you learn about inventions, does it make you want to learn more science?

Look what I can do!

- ☐ I can investigate different ways we use electricity.
- ☐ I can sort and group different types of switches.
- ☐ I can find the answer to questions by using books and the internet.

6 Electricity

> 6.2 Keep safe with electricity

We are going to:
- find out how to keep safe with electricity
- collect observations and write them in a table
- make predictions about what we think will happen.

Getting started
- What could happen to this child?
- How can we make her **safe**?

electric shock
protect
safe
wall socket

6.2 Keep safe with electricity

Electricity can be very dangerous if you don't take care.

Electricity is safe if you follow the rules.

Electricity Safety Rules

1. Children should not move or touch mains appliances, wires or plugs.
2. Children should not touch mains wall sockets.
3. Keep water away from electrical appliances.
4. Keep dirt away from electrical appliances.
5. Keep away from damaged wire and damaged electrical appliances.
6. Do not open or burn electrical cells.

Electricity moves through the metal part of a wire.

The metal should be covered by plastic. The plastic is to **protect** you.

plastic

metal

Never touch damaged wires. They could give you an electric shock.

Electricity could burn or kill you if you touched these wires.

6 Electricity

Never stick anything into an electric wall socket.
The metal parts inside could give you an electric shock.

Mains electricity can move through water.

Never touch anything that uses mains electricity with wet hands.

6.2 Keep safe with electricity

Electricity can move though dust and dirt.

Keep dust or dirt away from **wall sockets** and mains electricity.

Never touch dirty or damaged electrical things.

Broken cells can burn your skin and hurt your eyes.

Never put a cell in a fire. Never touch an open cell.

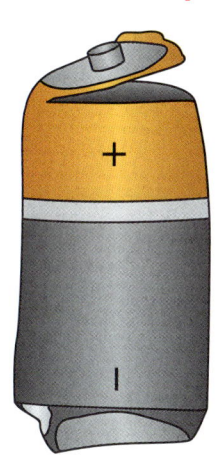

Questions

1. What might happen to you if you touch an electric wall socket with wet hands?
2. What might happen if you touch a broken cell?

6 Electricity

Activity 1

Mains means danger

Your teacher will show you a mains-powered appliance.

The wire and plug mean that this appliance is mains-powered.

Now work with a friend to write some rules for children about mains-powered appliances.

Activity 2

Electrical safety poster

Make an electrical safety poster which tells others how to stay safe with electricity.

6.2 Keep safe with electricity

Think like a scientist

Electrical safety survey

Ask some children from another class the questions shown in this table.

Do you predict that they will know these things?

Record their answers like this.

Questions for children about electrical safety. We got answers from 15 children	yes	no	don't know
Q1 Are young children allowed to plug appliances into a mains wall socket?	5	7	3
Q2 Should you touch an electrical appliance with wet hands?			
Q3 Should we keep electrical things clean?			
Q4 Can electricity hurt you?			

What answers did you get? Are all the children safe?

Were your predictions right?

Give your results to the teacher of these children.

Ask their teacher to tell their class about electrical safety.

How am I doing?

Tell a friend how mains electricity can hurt you.

6 Electricity

You don't need to be scared of electricity, but electricity can hurt you. Does it help you to learn when you know about danger?

Look what I can do!

- ☐ I can find out about how to keep safe with electricity.
- ☐ I can collect observations onto a table.
- ☐ I can say what I think will happen.

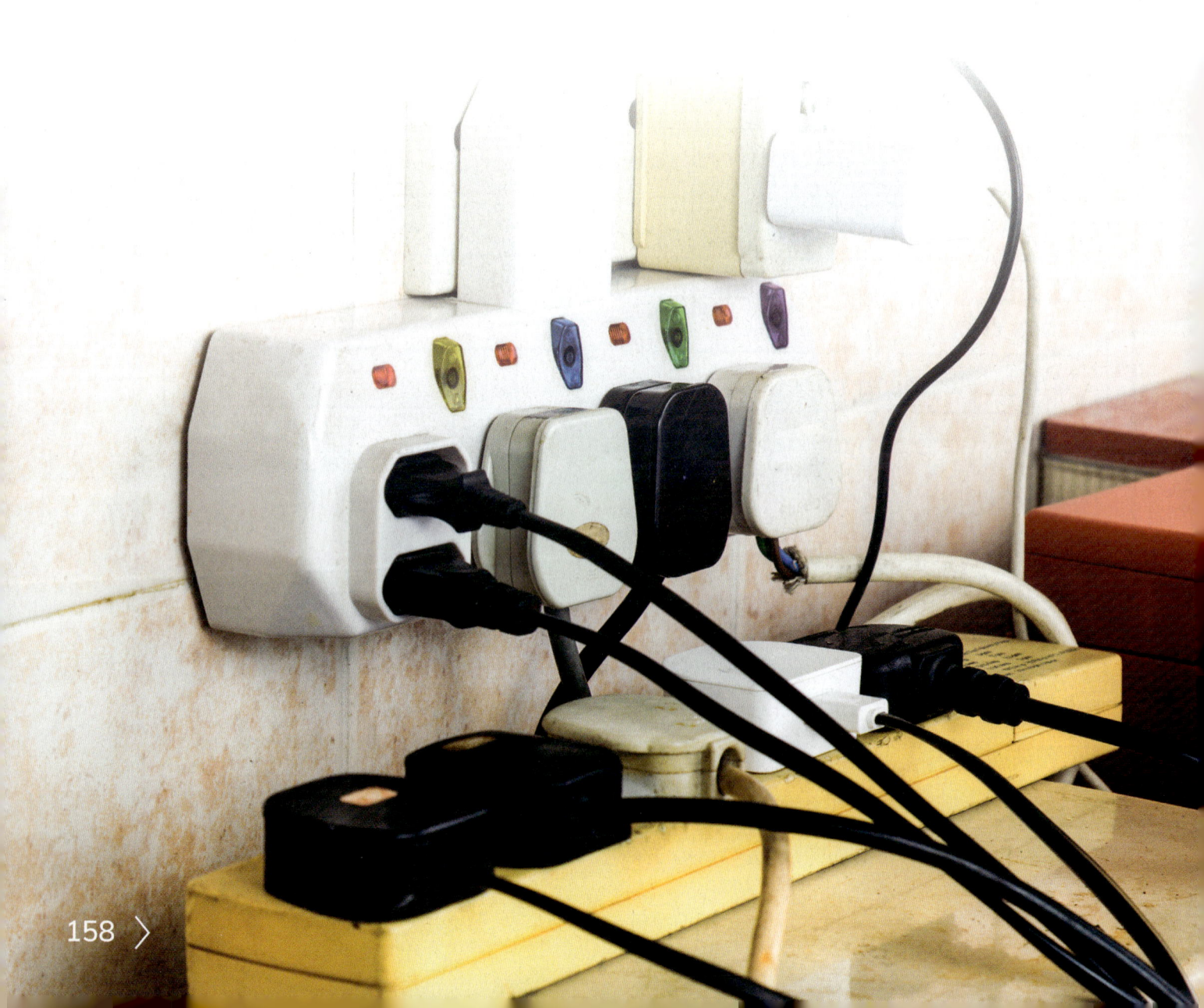

> 6.3 Making circuits

We are going to:
- explore making different circuits with cells, wires and lamps
- make predictions and see if they were right
- find patterns in results
- follow instructions safely when making circuits.

Getting started
- Talk about the parts inside this computer. Find the wires and fans. Why are there wires inside the computer?

circuit
complete
conductor
connect
connection
flow
lamp

6 Electricity

You are going to use the things shown here to make an electrical **circuit**. A circuit is a path for the electricity to move along and make things work.

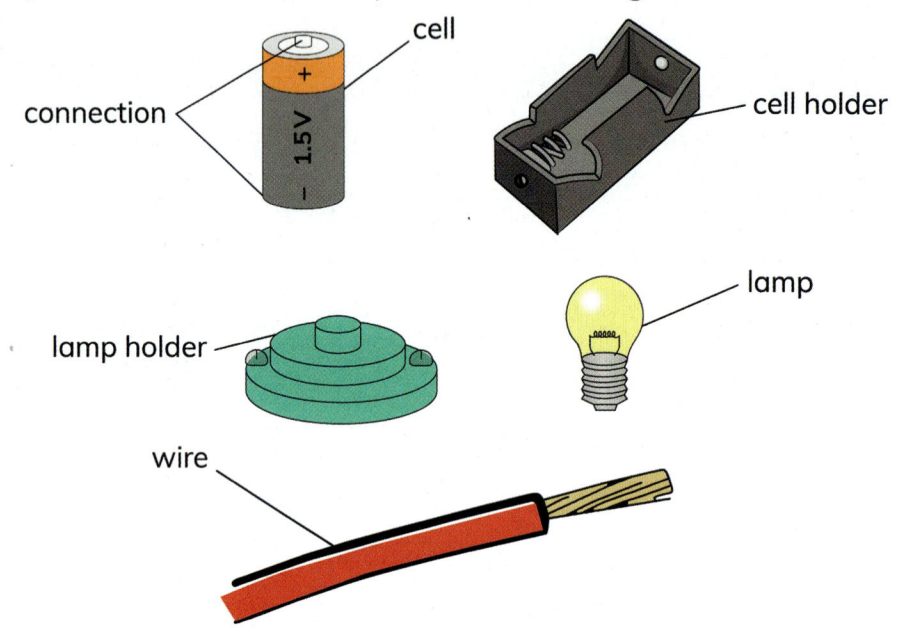

Each cell has two **connections** and both are used in a circuit.
The cell holder holds the cell and **connects** the cell to the wires.

The lamp holder holds the **lamp** and connects the lamp to the wires.

The lamp will shine when it is in a **complete** circuit.

This picture shows an electrical circuit. The metal part of the wire will carry electricity.

The arrows show how the electricity **flows** around the circuit.

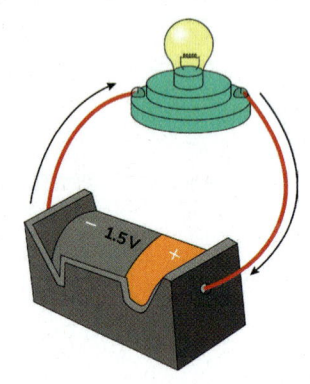

With a finger, follow the flow of the electricity from the cell around the circuit and back to the cell.

6.3 Making circuits

> **Activity 1**
>
> **Make a circuit**
>
> > **You will need:**
> > a cell, cell holder, two wires, a lamp and lamp holder
>
> Make a complete working circuit.
>
> Use your finger to follow the flow of electricity around the complete circuit.
>
> Try to break the circuit and stop it working.
>
> Now make the circuit work again.
>
> How do you know that you have made a complete circuit?

Some circuits don't work

These circuits are not working.

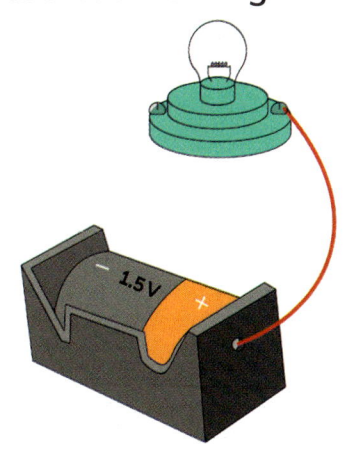

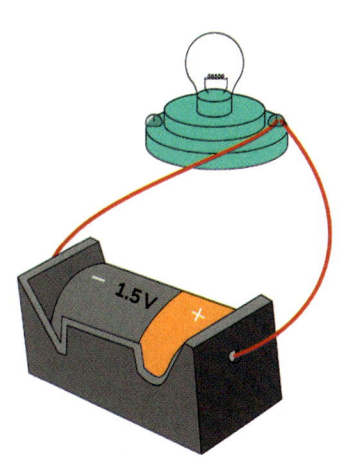

Question

1 Try to say why these two circuits won't work.

6 Electricity

Testing that a lamp works

We can test that a lamp is working.
We use two wires and a cell like this. This is a complete circuit.

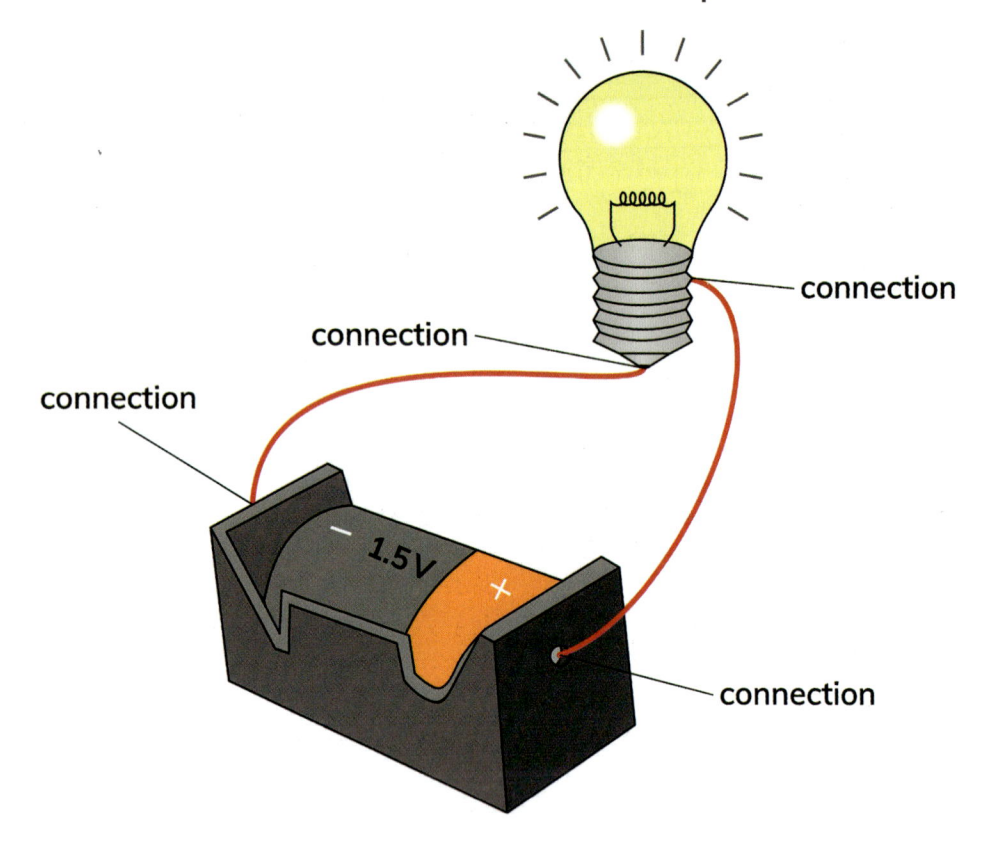

connection
connection
connection

1.5 V

Think like a scientist

Do more lamps mean brighter lamps?

You will need:
two cells, two cell holders, wires, 3 lamp holders,
3 lamps, wires, crocodile clips

Make a circuit with two cells, wires, one lamp holder and one lamp.

6.3 Making circuits

Continued

Predict what will happen to the brightness of the lamp if you add more lamps to the circuit.

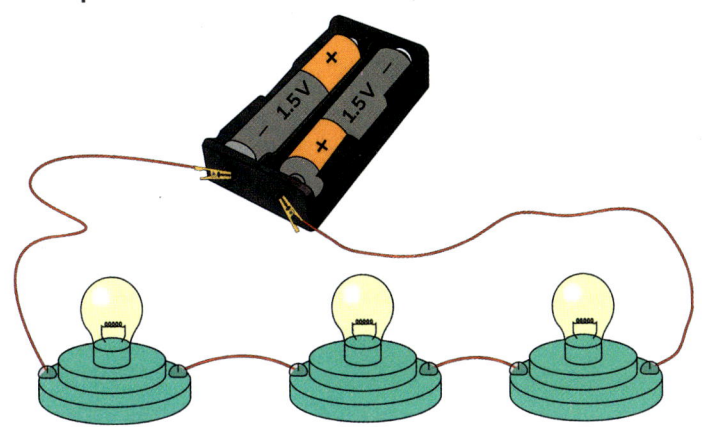

Complete the table below.

number of lamps	I predict that…	I noticed…
1	the lamp will be bright	the lamp was bright
2		
3		

What happened when you added the lamps?

Was your prediction right? Do you notice a pattern?

Metal is a conductor

Electricity flows along the metal part of a wire.

Metal is a conductor of electricity.

Some materials like plastic do not conduct electricity.

The plastic on the outside of the wire keeps us safe.

Question

2 What would happen if mains wires did not have a plastic covering?

6 Electricity

Activity 2

Why are wires made of metal?

You will need:
a cell, a cell holder, wires, a lamp holder, a lamp, materials to test, crocodile clips

Make a circuit like this.

The circuit is not complete so electricity will not flow.

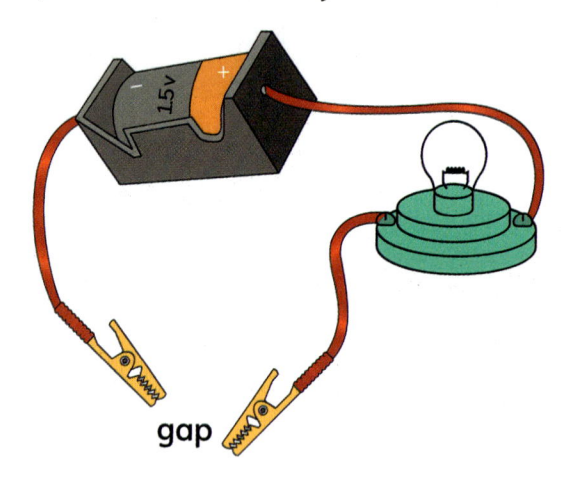

gap

Now use this circuit to test materials. Place the material into the gap and hold the wires onto it to complete the circuit. If the material conducts electricity, the lamp will light up.

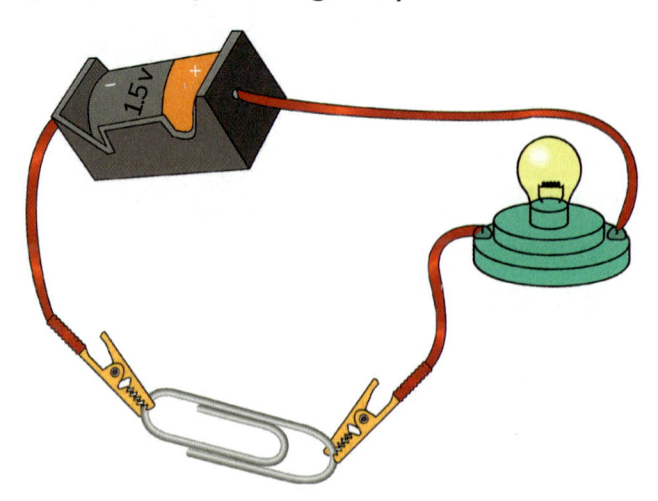

6.3 Making circuits

Continued

Predict which materials will conduct electricity.
Test them and record your results. Use a table like this.

Material	Will it conduct electricity?	
	prediction	result
metal foil	no	yes

Did you find materials that conducted electricity?

Did you see a pattern in the results?

Copper is a good conductor of electricity, so we use it in electrical wires.

Activity 3

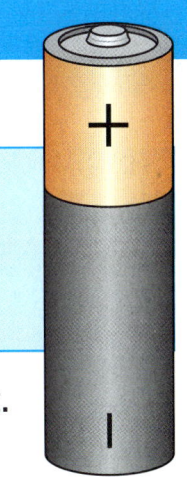

Do more cells make lamps brighter?

> **You will need:**
> wires and crocodile clips, two cells, two cell holders, lamp holder, lamp

Use one cell, wires, a lamp holder and a lamp to make a circuit.

Check that it works.

Predict what will happen if you add another cell to the circuit.

Now add the second cell and observe what happens.

Make sure both cells are the same way around.

Was your prediction right?

6 Electricity

Continued

How am I doing?

You have made electrical circuits.

Tell a friend why the connections were important.

You can't see electricity. Do you find it harder to learn about things that you cannot see? Why?

Look what I can do!

- ☐ I can use wires, cells, lamps to make electrical circuits.
- ☐ I can make predictions and see if they were right.
- ☐ I can find patterns in results.
- ☐ I can follow instructions safely when making circuits.

Project: Invent a new electrical appliance

People invent new appliances every day.
Many new appliances use electricity.

Could you invent an appliance to:

- take your pet for a walk?

- play ball with you?

- add lights to your shoes?

Perhaps you have another idea?

Draw your idea for a new electrical appliance.

Does your appliance use cells or mains electricity?

Does your appliance have a switch?

Say what your appliance does.

6 Electricity

Check your progress

Talk about the answers to these questions with your classmates.

1   Name these things.

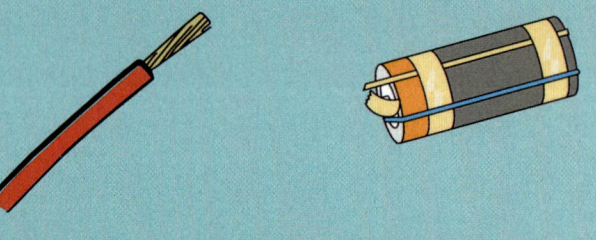

2   Are these things safe or dangerous?

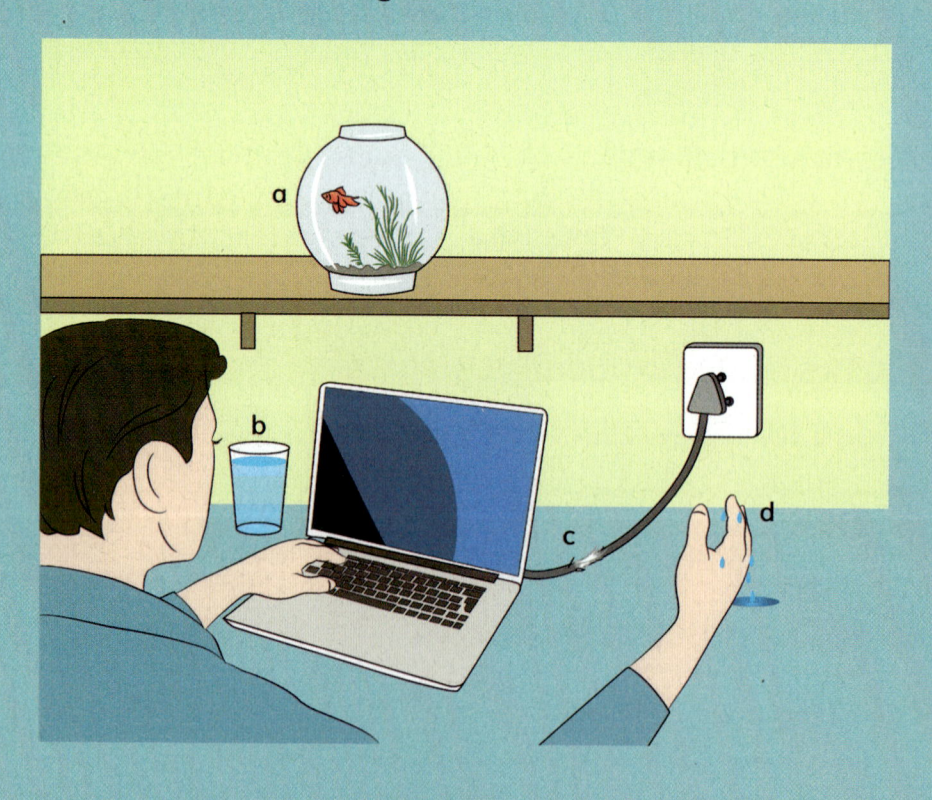

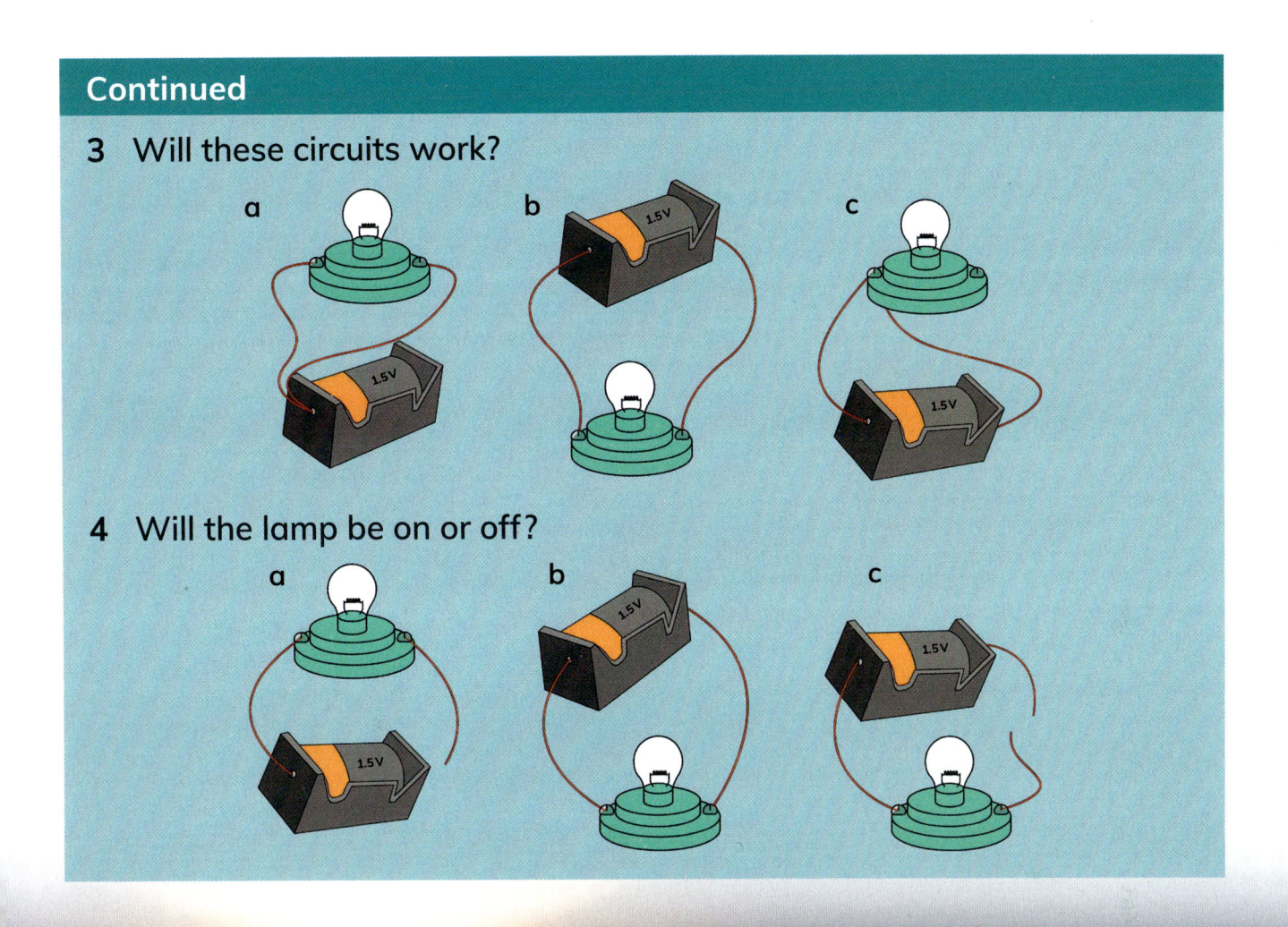

Check your progress

Continued

3 Will these circuits work?

a   b   c

4 Will the lamp be on or off?

a   b   c

Science skills

Science skills

How to draw a block graph

Zara and Marcus have done a fair test to find out which cushion is the softest.

They used a ruler and some bricks to measure how soft each cushion was.

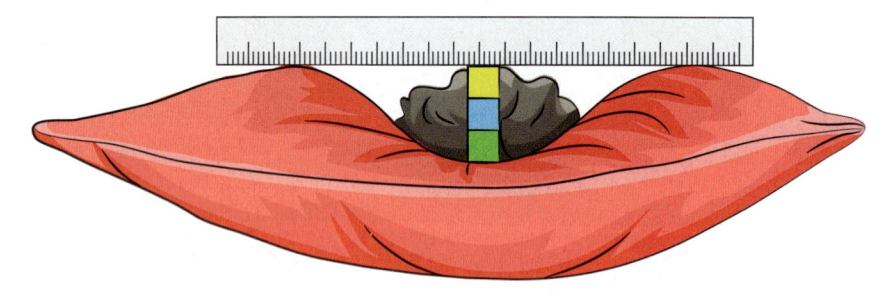

Here are their results.

Cushion	Numbers of bricks
green	5
red	3
blue	2

They used their results to make a block graph.

Marcus fills in the block graph for the green cushion.

The number of bricks was five, so he colours five of the blocks on the graph.

Science skills

Zara colours three blocks on the graph for the red cushion and two blocks for the blue cushion.

The block graph makes the results easy to understand.

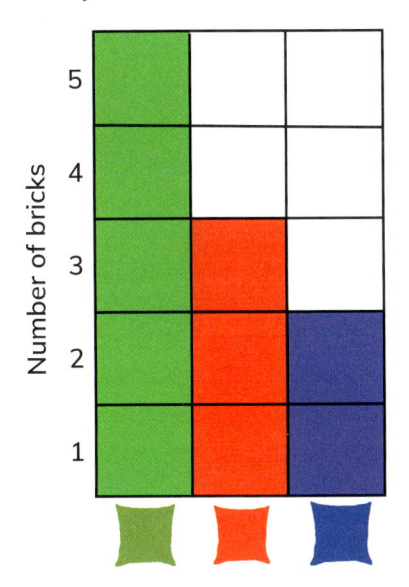

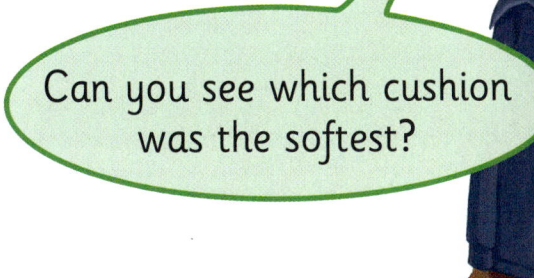

Can you see which cushion was the softest?

Science skills

How to stay safe in the Sun

The children are sharing ideas on how the Sun appears to move across the sky.

How can they stay safe?

The Sun is very bright. Looking at it will damage your eyes.

Take care with other bright light sources. They can also damage your eyes.

Science skills

How to stay safe in the kitchen

When you try to answer a science question, you must think about what could go wrong. You must think about how to stay safe.

Zara wants to know how materials change when they are heated.

She is not being safe.

What dangers can you see?

What might happen? How can Zara stay safe?

Only work in a kitchen if you have an adult to help you.

Always put sharp knives somewhere safe.

A cooker gets very hot. Keep your hands and other objects away from the heat.

Keep electrical appliances away from water or you could get an electric shock.

Science skills

How to stay safe online

You might want to use the internet to look for the answer to a science question.

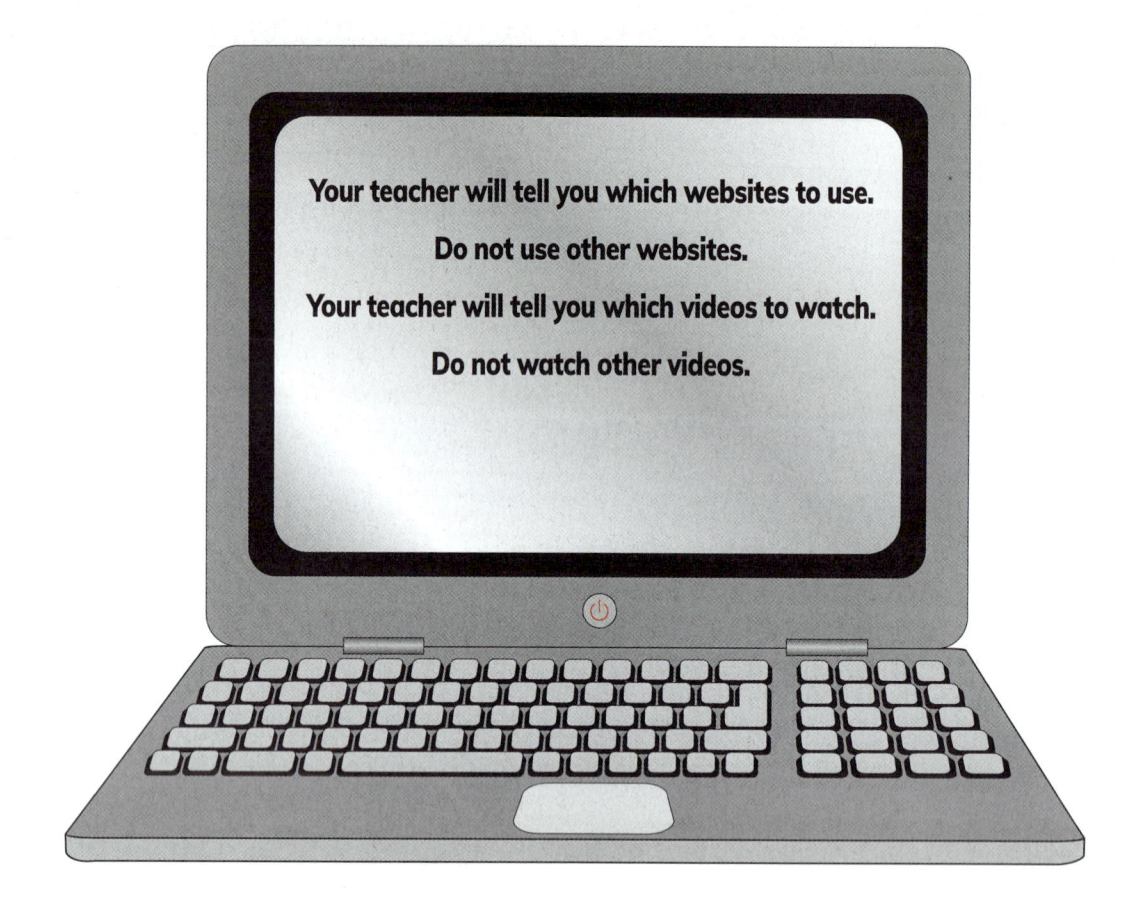

Your teacher will tell you which websites to use.

Do not use other websites.

Your teacher will tell you which videos to watch.

Do not watch other videos.

Glossary and index

absorb	when water soaks into the material	23
absorbent	something that soaks up water and other liquids, not waterproof	66
adult	an animal that is fully grown and could become a parent	95
age	how many years a living thing has been alive	97
attract	draw something towards it	17
away	moving away from something is getting less close to it	37
baby	a very young animal	94
bird	an animal with feathers and wings, most birds can fly	90
block graph	a way of showing results that uses squares or blocks instead of numbers	74
brakes	the parts of a bike or other vehicle that make it slow down	47
bright	a bright object gives off a lot of light, opposite to dull	124
calcium	something found in milk and other dairy food that helps teeth grow strong	113
calf	a young elephant, cow or whale is called a calf	95
canine	a type of tooth with a pointed top for gripping food	115

cell (electrical)	a source of energy or electricity that can power a circuit	148
characteristics	what a material or a living thing is like, for example, a material could be flexible or rigid, an animal could have two legs or four legs	65
chick	young birds are called chicks	96
circuit	a circle of joined wire and electrical parts along which electricity flows	160
clean	not dirty	110
clues	things we observe which help us understand	14
compare	to look at two things and find things that are similar and different	5
complete	no missing parts	160
conductor	a material through which electricity will flow	163
connect	to join things together	160
connection	a place where things (for example, two wires) join together	160
cotton	a fluffy white material that comes from a plant and is made into a fabric	62
crack	a broken part of a material	8
cub	a young bear, wolf, lion or tiger is called a cub	96
dairy	food that has milk in it or food that is made from milk	113
dangerous	it may hurt you	147

dark	less light or no light	131
daylight	the light we get from the Sun	138
dentist	a doctor who looks after people's teeth	113
describe	use words to say what something is like	12
desert	a very dry place with little or no living things	8
diagram	a drawing that shows important information and explains this with labels and arrows, lines and text	54
diet	the food we eat	107
direction	a path towards or away from something	53
discovery	something found for the first time	150
droppings	solid waste made by animals	14
dull	something that light does not bounce off, not shiny	68
egg	a shell or case made by female animals, each contains young	15
electric shock	a dangerous amount of electricity in a person's body	153
electrical appliance	a device that uses electricity to work	146
electricity	we use it to make things work like TVs, computers, phones	146
environment	the natural and made space and things around you	2
exercise	moving around using your muscles	110
explain	to make something clear	50
explosive	a material that will blow things apart	24

fast, faster	to take little time to move to a new place	47
feathers	feathers cover the skins of birds and help them to fly	90
fingerprint	the pattern of lines in the skin of your fingers	103
flashlight	an electric light that you can hold in your hand	124
flexible	something that can bend, squash or twist, not rigid	65
flow	move	160
fluoride	something found in some toothpastes which makes teeth stronger	113
force	a push or a pull	37
fur	soft hair that covers the skin of some animals	89
germs	very small living things that can make you ill	108
glass	a clear material we use to make windows	61
gravel	small pieces of rock	25
grow/growth	changes that happen as living things get older	95
gums	the part of the mouth that teeth grow from	115
habitat	the place a living thing finds everything it needs to grow and have young	2
headache	when your head hurts	108
heart	part of our bodies that pumps blood around our body to help keep us alive	110
height	how far from the bottom to the top of an object	43

hide	keeping out of sight	14
home	the place an animal sleeps, feels safe and cares for its young	3
human	a person	89
identical	exactly the same	102
ill/illness	not feeling well, not being well	107
incisor	a type of tooth with a flat sharp top for biting food	115
information	facts about something	81
inherit	getting a characteristic from a parent when you are born	102
insect	a small animal with three body parts and six legs	17
invention	something new created by a person	150
investigate	to do a test or experiment to find something out	45
label	words added to a picture to give information	4
lamp	gives light when it is in a circuit	160
launch	when something starts moving into the air or into water	40
light source	an object which makes light	123
liquid	a material that can flow and be poured, for example, water is a liquid	79
litter	something dropped on the ground which should be put in a bin	27
local	the area around you	4

mains electricity	very powerful electricity we use in buildings	147
mammal	an animal that has hair or fur and has live babies instead of laying eggs	89
material	a substance used to make something	30
measure	to find the size or amount of something, for example length or time	43
melt	to change from solid to liquid	79
mine	hole dug to extract rocks or minerals	24
mixture	something that is made by putting different materials together	79
model	a copy we make (often smaller) of a real thing	5
molar	a type of tooth with a wide lumpy top for chewing food	115
Moon	large body which orbits Earth and which, on most nights, reflects light to Earth	124
muscles	part of our bodies that can make us move	110
natural	can be found in nature, not made by people	60
nature reserve	a place which is made to be a good habitat for plants and animals	30
night time	the hours of darkness	131
object	something made of a material that you can see or touch.	43
oil	a black liquid material that is found underground that can burn	60
old/older	an animal that has been alive for a long time	95

paper	a material we can use to write on	61
parent	an animal's mother or father	94
pattern	a change that is similar each time	44
pedals	the parts of a bike you push with your feet to make it move	47
photograph	a picture made by a camera	8
pictogram	a way of showing results that uses pictures instead of numbers	99
plastic	a material that comes in many different colours and shapes	61
plug	a connection to mains electricity	147
position	an object's place in the physical world	140
power station	a factory that makes electricity	148
pretend	imagine something	10
property /properties	what something is like, for example, smooth and shiny are properties of glass	64
protect	to take care of something or someone	29
pull/pulls	to try to move something towards you	36
push/pushes	to try to move something away from you	36
quarry	a place where the surface rocks are removed so that rock from just below the surface can be dug out	24
record	to draw or write what happened	8
recycle	reuse a material so that it does not get dumped	29

reflect	light changing direction after hitting a surface	124
results	what you observe or measure in an investigation	44
rigid	something that keeps its shape and is not easy to bend, squash or twist, not flexible	65
robot	an appliance that can do things by following instructions	146
rock	a hard material that comes from the Earth's surface	19
rocked	something that moves from side to side	149
rocket	something that can fly to into space	40
rough	something is bumpy, not flat, not smooth	67
rubber	a material that can bend easily and comes from the rubber tree	60
safe	not dangerous	152
sample	a piece of a material	22
sand	loose yellow or brown material made up of very small pieces of rock	60
scare	frighten	15
shape	the outline of an object, for example, square, curved or flat	42
shine	making or reflecting light	124
shiny	something that light bounces off, not dull	68
sick	being sick is when your body pushes everything in your tummy out through your mouth	108

slide	to move something from side to side	149
slow down, get slower	when something starts to move less quickly	47
slow, slower	to take a long time to move to a new place	47
smooth	something that is flat, not bumpy, not rough	67
solid	a material that keeps its shape and does not flow	79
speed	how fast something is moving	47
speed up, get faster	when something starts to move more quickly	47
squashing	changing the shape of a material by pushing, when something gets shorter	40
star	a very large burning object in the sky which is very far away and so appears very small	138
stones	small rocks	25
stretch	change the shape of a material by pulling, when something gets longer	39
stripes	a pattern of lines	102
strong	something that is not easy to break, not weak	66
sundial	a device which casts a shadow indicating the time of day	140
sweat	when your skin become wet because you are hot or ill	110
swirl	make a liquid spin	26
switch	a device to control the flow of electricity (on/off)	149
table	a grid of squares we use to write or draw results	15

toothpaste	something to put on a toothbrush to help clean teeth and make them strong	113
towards	moving towards something is getting closer to it	37
tracks	marks made by an animal as it moves	14
transparent	a material you can see through clearly	70
turn	when something moving changes to move on a different path	53
twins	two people or animals with the same mother who were born at the same time	103
Venn diagram	a picture used for sorting with two or more circles that overlap	67
wall socket	the place you connect some electrical appliances to the mains	155
water	a clear liquid material that we need to drink, the sea and rivers are water	60
waterproof	a material that does not let water through	21
weak	something that is easy to break, not strong	66
wire	a long thin piece of metal	147
wood	a material that comes from the trunk of a tree	60
young (adj)	an animal that has not been alive for long	95
young (noun)	an animal's babies are called its young	95

Acknowledgements

The authors and publishers acknowledge the following sources of copyright material and are grateful for the permissions granted. While every effort has been made, it has not always been possible to identify the sources of all the material used, or to trace all copyright holders. If any omissions are brought to our notice, we will be happy to include the appropriate acknowledgements on reprinting.

Thanks to the following for permission to reproduce images:

Cover by Pablo Gallego (Beehive Illustration); **Inside** Unit 1 Georgette Douwma/GI; Lydie Gigerichova/GI; KenCanning/GI; GeoStock/GI; GK Hart/Vikki Hart/GI; Ron and Patty Thomas/GI; Mirben Igot / EyeEm/GI; Alex Potemkin/GI; PamelaJoeMcFarlane/GI; Matteo Colombo/GI; Ruben Earth/GI; Image Source/GI; Hiindy22/GI; Images Of Our Lives/GI; janetteasche/GI; Klaus Vartzbed/GI; oxygen/GI; Mint Images/GI; Germán Vogel/GI; Joe Sohm/Visions of America/Universal Images Group/GI; Cultura RM Exclusive/Kevin C Moore/GI; Aaron Geddes Photography/GI; VvoeVale/GI; Tim Grist Photography/GI; MassanPH/GI; Magnetcreative/GI; A_Pobedimskiy/GI; Vm/GI; Andresr/GI; Deepspace/GI; Mac99/GI; Gallo Images-Denny Allen/GI; Sarayut Thaneerat/GI; Manop Boonpeng/GI; Lane Oatey/GI; Anton Petrus/GI; © Nora Carol Photography/GI; Dgwildlife/GI; Leland Bobbe/GI; GerardJacob/GI; Thorney Lieberman/GI; Magnetcreative/GI; Unit 2 Zia Soleil/GI; Skynesher/GI; SDI Productions/GI; Lorado/GI; Nick Dolding/GI; Nick David/GI; ilona75/GI; Ross Woodhall/GI; A Rey/GI; Kelly Cheng Travel Photography/GI; Peter Muller/GI; Greg Pease/GI; Zbruch/GI; Hdagli/GI; South_agency/GI; Mint Images/GI; Nattrass/GI; Unit 3 MassanPH/GI; Lisa Lemanczyk/EyeEm/GI; Andrew Merry/GI; WLADIMIR BULGAR/SCIENCE PHOTO LIBRARY/GI; Chonticha wat/GI; westphalia/GI; James Hardy/GI; Lilly Husbands/GI; Monty Rakusen/GI; Monty Rakusen/GI; Jurgita Vaicikeviciene/GI; Busakorn Pongparnit/GI; Idrees Abbas/SOPA Images/LightRocket/GI; Daniel Grill/Tetra Images/GI; FotografiaBasica/GI; Peter Schaefer/EyeEm/GI; Dermot Conlan/GI; Gary S Chapman/GI; Azat Anbekov/EyeEm/GI; TS Photography/GI; Ballyscanlon/GI; Luoman/GI; Boonchai wedmakawand/GI; Unit 4 Mantaphoto/GI; AB Photography/GI; Daniel Hernanz Ramos/GI; Dantesattic/GI; 1001slide/GI; Andyd/GI; Mvp64/GI; Peter Augustin/GI; Tunart/GI; nadtytok/GI; Paul Taylor/GI; Manoj Shah/GI; Steve Allen/GI; Hiphotos35/GI; monkeybusinessimages/GI; Evgenii Zotov/GI; Rajbir Sunny Oberoi/500px/GI; CP Cheah/GI; Cheryl Bronson/GI; Layland Masuda/GI; SCIEPRO/SCIENCE PHOTO LIBRARY/GI; Alan Powdrill/GI; Santiago Iñiguez/EyeEm/GI; Somethingway/GI; Maskot/GI; Peter Cade/GI; John Giustina/GI; Milan Markovic/GI; Martin Harvey/GI; Paul Starosta/GI; Rodrigo Friscione/GI; wilpunt/GI; Unit 5 Pat Law Photography/GI; NASA/GI; LEON NEAL/AFP/GI; Andrew Bret Wallis/GI; Michael Betts/GI; Grinvalds/GI; FSTOPLIGHT/GI; JGI/Jamie Grill/GI; Yulia-Images; Fstop123/GI; Spike Mafford/GI; Donald Iain Smith/GI; John S Lander/LightRocket/GI; Gillianne Tedder/GI; Ansel Siegenthaler/GI; EyeEm/GI; Photos.com/GI; Stockcam/GI; Tammy616/GI; Bettmann/GI; Unit 6 Photo12/Universal Images/GI; Zhongguo/GI; Graphicassault/GI; Difydave/GI; ET-ARTWORKS/GI; MicroStockHub/GI; Flubydust/GI; RapidEye/GI; Hulton Archive/GI; Westersoe/GI; Demarco-media/GI; Jevtic/GI; kvsan/GI; Elizabeth Fernandez/GI; Tsvi Braverman/GI.

Key: GI= Getty Images